D1435517

THE NATURE *of* HAPPINESS

THE NATURE
of HAPPINESS

DESMOND MORRIS

Little Books by Big Names™

To Ramona, who has made me happy
for over half a century.

First published in the United Kingdom in 2004 by Little Books Ltd,
48 Catherine Place, London SW1E 6HL

10 9 8 7 6 5 4 3 2 1

A CIP catalogue record for this book is available from the British Library.

ISBN: 1 904435 28 9

The author and publisher will be grateful for any information that will assist them
in keeping future editions up-to-date. Although all reasonable care has been taken in the
preparation of this book, neither the publisher, editors nor the author can accept any liability
for any consequences arising from the use thereof, or the information contained therein.

Many thanks to: Jamie Ambrose for editorial production and management,
Mousemat Design Limited for jacket and text design, Imago for printing consultancy.
Printed and bound in China.

CONTENTS

INTRODUCTION

One sure way to make me unhappy is to lecture me on how to make my life happier. You will gather from this that *The Nature of Happiness* is not one of those 'self-improvement tracts' that tries to bully you into a routine of happiness-increasing exercises, or attempts to enrol you on courses of happiness-coaching. Nor will it aid you in 'assessing your enduring happiness with a general happiness questionnaire'.

What it does do is to provide an explanation of the various sources of happiness. If, in this way, it helps you to understand the elusive emotional condition that we refer to in ordinary speech as 'being happy', then it is that understanding that may eventually help you to live a happier life. In other words, this book does not preach to you, insisting that you behave in a certain way to gain happiness, but rather gives you knowledge that you can use, if you wish, to make you happier. There is more than one way of achieving happiness and each has its strengths and its weaknesses. Some ways will appeal to you and some will not.

The people who run classes in 'increasing your chances of lasting happiness' might well be surprised by questions such as: 'Why does cocaine make a drug-addict happy?' 'Why does blowing people to bits bring a state of blissful happiness to a suicide-bomber?' or 'Why does inflicting pain create a surge of happiness in a sadist?' And yet these are all valid queries if one is to understand the true nature of happiness. Every kind of happiness must be considered – even those that most of us view as repulsive, anti-social or dangerous. Only when we scan the whole range of possibilities can we hope to get to grips with the truth of this complex phenomenon.

THE SOURCE OF HAPPINESS

The true nature of happiness is frequently misunderstood. It is often confused with contentment, satisfaction or peace of mind. The best way to explain the difference is to describe contentment as the mood when life is good, while happiness is the sensation we experience when life suddenly gets better. At the very moment when something wonderful happens to us, there is a surge of emotion, a sensation of intense pleasure, an explosion of sheer delight – and this is the moment when we are truly happy. Sadly, it does not last very long. Intense happiness is a transient, fleeting sensation. We may continue to feel good for quite a while, but the joyful elation is quickly lost. As one cynic put it: life is prolonged misery interrupted by brief moments of happiness.

So what causes these brief interludes? To find the answer we have to look back at the way our species evolved over a million years. Our remote ancestors were tree-dwellers feeding mostly on fruits, nuts and insects. Like other monkeys, they did not experience many peak moments in their day-to-day lives. But then they took a new evolutionary route, away from that of their close relatives. They abandoned the more gentle, repetitive, fruit-picking way of life in the trees and took to the more strenuous, demanding lifestyle of pack-hunters on the plains. This switch demanded a new mental attitude. There had to be an increase in cooperation, communication, intelligence, courage, and the ability to concentrate for long periods of time on a specific goal.

The cooperation was needed to defeat powerful prey animals. Communication was needed to plan hunting strategies and organize the tactics of the chase and kill. Courage was required; for a puny primate to attempt to become a lethal predator required serious risk-taking of a kind alien to our monkey forebears. At the first sign of danger, the typical reaction of a monkey is to flee up into the safety of the trees. Our ancestors had to repress those panic responses and face up to the hazards of hunting in an entirely new way. Concentration was needed because, compared with picking a fruit, killing prey is a long-term activity. Our ancestors had to develop concerted, focused persistence of a kind also new to primates.

In order to carry out this dangerous new feeding pattern successfully, we also had to become much more athletic: hungry for vigorous physical activity. Once triumphant, another new element had to be introduced into our social life – we had to develop food-sharing. For some reason best known to their personal therapists, Hollywood film producers always seem to want to portray prehistoric man as a viciously competitive, savagely violent being, forever clubbing his companions over the head in eternal tribal squabbles. Of course, such incidents occasionally took place, and still do, but if they had been the order of the day we could never have survived as a species in the earliest phase of our evolution. Violence within the group had to be the exception to the rule, or there would have been chaos. The dominant mood must have been one of mutual aid, cooperation and sharing. Without it, we could never have prospered.

Reading our newspapers today and watching our television screens, we get the impression that we live in brutal, violent times. But this is a distortion of the truth almost as great as that of the Hollywood producers who gave us the ug-ug, thump-thump version of our primeval ancestors. If we take into account the population levels we have attained and the extreme level of over-crowding to which we are now exposed, we are really an astonishingly peaceful, amicable species. If you doubt this, try counting the thousands of millions of human beings who woke up this morning and made it through the day without punching someone in the face. Luckily for our species, most people are like that. Luckily for the newscasters, there is a tiny minority of the 6,000 million of us who do, on rare occasions, throw a brick or explode a bomb — enough, at any rate, to keep the newscast filled. But we must never lose sight of the fact that the vast majority of us, for most of the time, are much more concerned with the quest for happiness rather than indulging in some kind of cruelty.

Another consequence of our switch to a hunting way of life was a dramatic increase in our curiosity. We developed an almost obsessional urge to explore and investigate the world around us. One sees this in the playfulness of young monkeys, but by the time they are adults it starts to fade. We, on the other hand, extend this childhood playfulness into adult life where it matures into an urge to analyze and classify the elements of our environment. Only in this way could we have developed the necessary knowledge of our tribal hunting grounds and the behaviour of our prey species. As a bonus, our intense curiosity led to inventiveness, our inventions led to innovations, and our innovations led to technological advances.

These technological advances eventually — after a million years or so of moulding as tribal hunters — took us over a startling new threshold. The primeval hunter became a farmer. By controlling our prey and modifying it to suit our needs, and by modifying our plant foods and controlling those, too, we reached a state about ten thousand years ago when, for the first time, we had a food surplus. Food-getting had become so efficient that it was no longer necessary for all members of the tribe to be involved in it. This meant that specialists could develop particular skills at a dramatic rate. This neolithic revolution saw villages grow into towns and towns into cities. The small tribal units became swollen into super-tribes. The powerful curiosity factor — humanity's great inventiveness — was now given full rein. Happiness meant a new toy, a new bauble, a new material, a new gadget, a new form of transport, a new style of building. Sadly, it also meant a new weapon and a new dungeon.

The peaceful, tribal hunter was now under consider-able pressure. Many of his behaviour patterns were strained to the limit by his new super-tribal existence. The urban ape was a nouveau riche and he made some terrible gaffes. His success story was running ahead of him and he found it hard to develop the new mentality needed for this novel way of life.

To start with, the delicate balance between competitiveness and cooperation was disturbed, swinging in favour of increased competition. The larger populations in the ancient towns and cities had become more impersonal. Bonds of friendship were being loosened. Those individuals who became local leaders were able to use their power with more ruthlessness than before. Slave classes emerged. For the majority, happiness went into a sharp decline. Even the glories of ancient Greece, whose praises we are so often singing, were based on a slave state.

Family relationships also suffered. In our long hunting phase we had made an important biological shift towards pair-bonding. In other words, our ancestors became programmed to fall in love. This was a vital step in the protection of the slow-growing young – especially when you recall that the males were away for long periods of time on the hunt and had to be tightly bonded to their females in order to return to the home base to feed and care for them and their offspring.

In the new urban structure, with specialization and division of labour having led to trading and bargaining as a way of life, it was inevitable that family ties would also become a matter of business rather than love. Arranged marriages became a new trading device. Love bonds that did not suit them were ruthlessly suppressed. More unhappiness spread in this important realm of intimate personal relations.

But the human animal is amazingly resilient. Every time new social trends began to pull us away from the central themes of our biological inheritance, some inner strength in our human nature helped to tug us back again. And the surprising feature of the last ten thousand years of the human story is that it has been a long struggle to return to a social condition similar to that in which we had existed in prehistoric times. Similar, but not, of course, the same. Each new technical advance has meant that we have had to find a new way of playing the game of being human.

I once described civilization as a first-aid kit carried on the shoulders of the naked ape, which was so heavy that it caused blisters on his feet — that required first aid. The naked ape, the human animal, is always trying to get back to its biological norm, but without giving up its new trappings.

We are aided in this delicate operation by an ability that stems from our linguistic developments. For we have become great symbolizers. We not only use symbolic speech, but also make symbolic equations in every sphere of our activities. And we are so good at symbolizing that we can experience an intense happiness from a symbolic success, a happiness just as real as if we were engaged in the original, primeval model of which the symbolic act is a copy.

To give a personal example, one of my great joys is going on a book-hunt. Finding a rare book I desperately want after a long search, acquiring it and carrying it home with me, is a symbolic equivalent of a primeval hunt for prey. Yes, I still need to hunt because I am human, but no, I do not have to kill a wild animal to satisfy my ancient biological hunting urge.

A vast proportion of the activities we engage in today are symbolic substitutes for the primeval hunt. This began as soon as the agricultural revolution removed hunting as a survival device. As soon as survival-hunting vanished, it was replaced by sport-hunting in which wild beasts were slaughtered as a pastime. The thrill of the chase was retained by the invention of blood sports. Later, when great towns and cities began to grow bigger and bigger, the urban population found itself unable to enjoy the chase, so the hunt was brought into the cities in a corrupted form: the arena display. The Coliseum was built in ancient Rome, and huge numbers of animals were brought there to be slain for the pleasure of the packed audience. On its opening day, nineteen hundred years ago, no fewer than five thousand animals perished. This form of slaughter became widespread and still lingers on in a modified form as the Spanish bullfight. And we all know about the annual bull-running in Pamplona, which dramatically recreates the dangers of the hunt. In many countries, sport-hunting still flourishes in a variety of forms, as though the civilizing process had never occurred. The hunting urge is so strong in us that even in the twenty-first century it can still explode in its bloody, original form, and people still need help to raise their symbolic equations to a more humane level.

Happily, the old arena blood sports have largely been replaced by arena ball sports. The squads of animal killers have been replaced by teams of sportsmen. Each ball sport has developed its own highly stylized version of the primitive hunt. In football, the prey has become a goal-mouth that has to be symbolically killed with a football. Because the target is too easy to hit with the missile, it has to be protected to make the game exciting. This protection is provided by the defending players of an opposing team. When enough goals have been scored (enough prey has been killed), the winning team of pseudo-hunters carries off a trophy and takes it back to their tribal headquarters, where it is displayed to their tribal followers from the balcony of the local town hall. This trophy, although inedible, sits symbolically on the table at the banquet that follows a great football triumph.

The hunting analogy is clear enough. The details have all changed, but the basic mood is still there: the planning and strategy, the tactics and dangers, the physical effort and injury, the group cooperation and, above all, the climactic aiming at a target. In fact, nearly all modern sports involve either aiming or chasing: the two fundamental elements of the primeval hunt.

If you want to watch the postures and expressions of intense, delirious happiness, watch the actions of the players and the fans when a last-minute winning goal is scored in an important match. I doubt if any primeval hunter ever leapt in the air with such abandoned joy. Modern sport has recreated in an abstract form a complex hunting sequence leading to rare moments of consummatory happiness.

For many of us, these sporting events may seem rather crude as sources of inspiring happiness. We may prefer more subtle and complex substitutes for the hunt. The businessman chooses to make a 'killing' in the city; the actor goes on stage to 'slay' his audience; the charity workers are delighted when they have raised enough money to meet their 'target'; the politician announces that to relieve the suffering of the poor is his 'aim'; the research scientist devotes his life to 'tracking dawn' a cure for cancer; the artist tries to 'trap' on canvas the perfect picture, and so on and so on.

The words we use to express our major motivations are revealing: killing, slay, target, aim, tracking down, trap. We are all symbolic hunters, wearing funny hats. Some of us wear several hats and find happiness in a variety of pursuits (and there is another hunting word: pursuit). Others prefer to specialize and may spend a whole lifetime doggedly chasing after a single prey.

Some types of symbolic hunt can take a whole lifetime. I am at present living in the house in which the *Oxford English Dictionary* was compiled by Sir James Murray. He spent over thirty years working on the huge dictionary and his goal, his ultimate prey, must have been to reach the end of the letter Z. It is with great sadness, a sense of a monumental happiness lost, that one discovers that he died at the letter T. He was working on the word 'turndown' at the time and never lived to experience the pure joy of completing the definition of 'zymurgy'. What a climactic moment of happiness that would have been.

Happiness means many things to different people, and yet I seem to have been dwelling largely on one type. I have been stressing the happiness that comes from satisfying our basic urge to hunt down prey, which has been transformed and elevated into so many fulfilling and creative pursuits today. I have done this because I believe that a great deal of the unhappiness we see now has been caused by a loss of this quality in the lives of so many of us. Those of us who have creative lives full of variety and challenge, with visible goals at which we can aim our efforts – we are the lucky ones. We can live in the way humans evolved to live: planning, striving, achieving, taking risks. But the agricultural revolution left a terrible blight on a large slice of humanity. Large numbers of individuals were, and in some countries still are, condemned to endless, boring, repetitive toil in the fields. The work was fit for grass-chewing cattle but not for intelligent, goal-oriented, inventive men and women.

With the industrial revolution, the situation grew worse. For the factory workers, there wasn't even a sky above them as they toiled. Their jobs became even more mindless, and any sort of end-product goal was beyond them. There was no joy to be had in such labour. We may have abolished the real slaves of ancient Greece, but all we did was to replace them with the wage-slaves of modern times. For them, moments of happiness had to be confined exclusively to activities outside their work. And yet it was their work that 'brought home the bacon'. In other words, it was their boring, repetitive work that was supposed to be substituting for the thrills of the primeval hunt. The major part of their lives was spent in activities that were insulting to the great brains that nestled inside their skulls: the greatest brains in the whole history of evolution. This terrible set-back for such a large slice of humanity meant that happiness had to be found in hobbies and holidays, in the corners of their lives rather than in its centre.

We are slowly correcting this now, but far too slowly. Eventually computer technology will replace the wage-slaves with unfeeling, mechanical slaves for most of the mind-numbingly simple duties, and it is the task of modern society to see that this has the effect of reducing the amount of boringly repetitive work to a minimum without reducing income. The increased efficiency of our advancing technologies should make this possible, but if we mishandle the situation we may end up with the nightmare of thousands put out of work by efficient, strike-proof robots. The possibility of a new golden age is there for the taking if only the world of politics could attract the more imaginative spirits among us. It is high time that that politicians took the trouble to find out what kind of animal species human beings belong to, and what makes them feel happy.

From this highly condensed history of our species, it is clear that there are a number of primary sources for human happiness. The first is what might be called 'Target Happiness' – the kind that stems from our ancient hunting past. There is also 'Competitive Happiness', the joy of winning, that is derived from our social background, as we evolved in small tribes. Opposed to this is 'Cooperative Happiness', based on our need to support one another to survive.

We did not lose our old biological urges – to eat, drink, mate and keep warm – and these are still present to give us our various forms of 'Sensual Happiness'. In addition, our increasingly complex brain gave us important sources of 'Cerebral Happiness', in which acts of intelligence became their own rewards.

These are some of the major categories of happiness and, together with a few others, they make up a simple classification of 'happiness-types'. It is worth examining them, one by one.

THE CLASSIFICATION
OF HAPPINESS

TARGET HAPPINESS
THE ACHIEVER

This has three stages: the anticipatory, the appetitive and the consummatory. Being the kind of animals we are — intensely curious, exploratory and inventive — we are constantly anticipating new projects, new experiences and new challenges, and their contemplation makes us happy. Then, when we start to work at them, if our work is challenging and varied, we enjoy the business of simply being busy and productive. Then, at the end of each venture, if we are successful, we can enjoy an almost orgasmic happiness with the sudden satisfaction we feel. A short pause and we are off again.

This is the hunter's happiness that stems from our evolutionary past as risk-taking predators, and it is clear that increasing the happiness of mankind in the future depends largely on finding more and more elegant ways of creating symbolic equivalents of the ancient hunting pattern with which to preoccupy our increasingly sophisticated populations. If we fail to do this and instead create boredom and frustration, then we may see more of the cruder, bloodstained substitutes. The choice is ours, but we must always remember that happiness is a fleeting, flitting, dynamic thing. As I said at the outset, happiness is not when things are good; it is when they are getting better.

One important aspect of target happiness concerns how high you set your sights. Some individuals aim too high and live out their lives in a more or less permanently soured, disappointed condition. This is the 'I could have been a concert pianist/pop-star/great actor if it hadn't been for my sick mother/children/demanding partner' syndrome.

Others aim too low and waste their talents. This is the 'I enjoy singing but I am not good enough to face an audience' syndrome. Lucky are the individuals who aim just high enough to match their potential.

The truth is that, since all our modern targets are symbolic, it really doesn't matter how grand or how modest our aims are, so long as they are ones we ourselves consider to be important. If a minor artist thinks he is a major artist, he will always be a failure to himself. And if a major artist thinks he is a minor artist, he too may fail because he never undertakes difficult, major works and never stretches himself to the full.

But if a minor artist knows he is a minor artist and accepts this truth, he may then be able to succeed in local art shows and achieve happiness at his modest level. If a major artist accepts that he has something great to offer, then he can drive himself on to undertake bigger and bigger challenges. And, for 'artist' you can read 'engineer,' or 'shopkeeper', or any other occupation.

COMPETITIVE HAPPINESS
The Winner

Because this has to do with reaching a triumphant conclusion, it is related to the last category, but there is a key difference. Target Happiness depends on reaching a personal goal, but not necessarily at the expense of a rival. With competitive happiness, winning is always at the expense of a rival, usually through the expenditure of huge effort. I am always amazed by the elated condition of a heavyweight boxer when he is interviewed immediately after winning a gruelling fifteen-round contest. The face that has been pummelled so brutally, with blow after jarring blow, is there on your television screen, in close-up, positively glowing with happiness and grinning inanely as though it had just seen a vision instead of a large gloved fist approaching repeatedly with the speed of light and the force of a sledge-hammer. It is a special kind of smile that we see on the faces of all winners, regardless of how they have just conquered their opponents, and it is almost impossible to imitate. I recall the painter Francis Bacon saying to me one day, 'I've got the scream alright, but I can't get the smile'. Qualities of smiling in moments of intense happiness are the hardest for artists and actors to capture, but they are quite unmistakable when we observe them.

The most vicious definition of happiness I have come across is the one that says, 'Happiness is an agreeable sensation arising from contemplating the misery of another.' If this makes us shudder, we should recall that every time we laugh at a joke we are guilty of a mild version of this, because in almost all jokes there is a victim whose discomfort amuses us, courtesy of one kind of banana-skin or another. A less worrying form of this definition is: 'Happiness is a pleasure not shared with others.' In both these cases we are dealing with competitive happiness, where we shamelessly or shamefully take our happiness from being one up.

The extreme form of this type of happiness is the most unpleasant kind of all. It is the happiness of the sadist and the torturer. For them, the infliction of pain on a helpless victim provides the ultimate surge of pleasure. It is the helplessness of the victim that is the key to their particular type of activity. If the victim can and does fight back, their pleasure is ruined. What they seek is complete subjugation. This instantly transforms the sadist or the torturer into the dominant figure in the relationship. This makes him the power-laden 'winner', and he continues to exploit this situation by inflicting pain on the victim. Each time he does this, the visible suffering of the victim re-enforces the torturer's feeling of power over another being. This is the coward's way of being a winner.

There are four main sources of happiness through cruelty: mental torture, physical torture, rape and murder. Mental torture all too often gives pleasure to a tyrannical individual who is in a position of social superiority. The arrogant tycoon, the callous boss, the higher military rank: all these can impose their cruelty on subordinates who are in no position to retaliate. These subordinates, in turn, attack their weaker companions in an attempt to regain their own self-respect after suffering humiliation. This has become known as 'the office-boy kicked the cat' syndrome, where cruelty starts at the top of a social hierarchy and ends at the bottom.

The most common victims are wives and children, who are too weak to fight back. In the United States, for example, where accurate records have been kept, it has emerged that there are over two million cases of battered women reported to the police annually. There are now fifteen hundred battered-women shelters in that country to provide sanctuaries for the worst cases. Fifty percent of the homeless women in America are refugees from domestic abuse. People living in happy families tend to think of this kind of violence as an extreme rarity. Sadly, it is not.

COOPERATIVE HAPPINESS
The Helper

This is the other side of the coin. We have always had to temper our competitiveness with cooperation because, as tribal animals, we could rarely succeed as isolated individuals. In addition to a deep-seated urge to win, we also inherited an equally basic, inborn urge to help one another. Moralists like to take credit for this, but the truth is that 'being helpful' is in our nature. It brings us happiness – not because do-gooders have taught us moral lessons in how to behave, but because biologically we are programmed to help ourselves by helping others.

Cooperative behaviour may appear to be selfless, but in reality it is just as selfish as competitive behaviour.

If we gain a surge of happiness from, say, helping our friends, this is because evolution has ensured that tribal members support one another as a defence against group failure. A single individual could not kill a large prey; nor could a single individual build a hut, make a feast, or protect a settlement. Individual members of the primeval group could only thrive if the whole tribe was successful, and this demanded active cooperation. Passive cooperation, obtained by threats and bullying, was not enough; we had to go one step further. Even the most dominant members of the tribe – those who had won the competitive struggles – had to offer rewards to their subordinates in order to keep the group working efficiently together.

In modern times, we see this cooperative urge at work in many different contexts. For most bosses, giving their staff a pay-rise or a bonus is a happy experience, whereas giving an employee the sack or a pay-cut is not. The ruthless boss, who, in wielding the carrot and stick, always favours the stick, will usually turn out to be a miserable individual, unable, for some personal reason, to enjoy the pleasures of cooperative happiness.

In trivial ways, small cooperative gestures can bring a strangely pleasing, fleeting moment of happiness — as when a driver in a traffic jam allows a car stuck in a side-street into the main flow of traffic. The wave of appreciation is worth a lot in that gridlocked sea of frustration.

On a grander scale, there is the widespread phenomenon of doing 'good works'. Some people, by symbolic means, are able to see the whole of humanity as members of their personal tribe. They can then set about helping their 'tribe' on a massive scale. All humanitarian organizations operate on this basis. The happiness they feel when providing food for a starving community on the other side of the world is based on their ability to see them as an extension of their own community. Officially they may claim to be operating according to some moral or religious code, but in reality they are obeying a modified form of an ancient, primeval 'cooperative imperative'. They are not being helpful because they have been taught to be helpful; they are being helpful because they belong to a helpful species.

There is an even more extreme version of this type of cooperative happiness. Many people are able to extend their compassion beyond humanity to other species. Conservationists spend their lives trying to protect certain kinds of animals from extinction, and animal welfare workers do their best to care for suffering domestic animals. Among such individuals, the passion for helping other species frequently becomes intense, and the great surge of happiness that occurs when a captive animal is returned to the wild, a rare animal is saved from extinction, a farm animal is given better living conditions, or an abandoned pet is found a new home, is immense. For these people, the symbolic equation is stretched to the limit, with the protected animals standing in for 'tribal members'.

Such is the power of human symbolic thought that we are able to widen our sources of happiness dramatically in this way. Strangely, however, when I interviewed people who are deeply involved in these activities, I soon discovered a weakness in their outlook. In theory they should be extremely cheerful individuals. They have increased their sources of cooperative happiness so greatly that they should find their lives immensely rewarding. In reality, however, they are often stressed and depressed instead of bubbling with the fun of 'being kind' on a grand scale.

I found a clear example of this when interviewing a woman who had devoted her whole life to saving stray cats. Over the years she had rescued literally thousands of felines from starvation, disease and lingering deaths. She had set up a huge sanctuary in which they were housed, given medical care and found new homes. Every cat saved and successfully re-housed should have given her a surge of happiness, but instead all she could think about were the cats she had failed to save. She was far from cheerful and was instead haunted by her failures, rather than made happy by her successes. This is the risk inherent in all such activities. The aims of the projects undertaken are so high that they can never be met. Another woman, horrified by the cruel treatment of a donkey that she observed when on holiday in North Africa, starting a project to save these delightful animals. She ended up with over three thousand of them on a huge farm complex, all of which had to be given medical attention and then had to be fed and cared for.

She was surrounded by healthy donkeys, a living testimony to her achievements in alleviating animal suffering, but all she could think about were the ones still waiting to be saved. Even if she bought them all and added hundreds of thousands of them to her farm, she could not succeed, because as soon as she paid for an abused donkey, its owner used the money to buy a young one and start again. Again, she had set herself an impossible task.

This is characteristic of all welfare activities. The surges of happiness are nearly always overpowered by pangs of sadness from the knowledge of what has not been achieved. The secret with cooperative happiness is to set oneself realistic goals, but this is hard to do. The reason for this difficulty is that the people or animals being helped are not real members of a small tribe of limited numbers, but symbolic equivalents of those tribal members. As symbols, their numbers are not limited by the natural tribe-size of the human species.

In primeval times, when evolution was laying down our inborn qualities, human tribes were very small. One estimate sees them as consisting of only eighty to a hundred and twenty individuals. At the very most they will only have consisted of a few hundred. At that scale, helpfulness is a practical possibility. Helping the whole of humanity, or the whole of the animal world, is another matter. To be success-fully enjoyed, cooperative happiness must find an appropriate scale.

This was brought home to me when I was involved in the making of a film about the problems of urbanization called *The Human Zoo*. I had argued that the enormous size of the city super-tribe had had the effect of increasing competitiveness and decreasing cooperation, dramatically unbalancing the relationship between these two basic human urges. In order to test this idea, we carried out a simple experiment on the streets of both big cities and small villages.

The producer of the film volunteered to fall down and lie inert on a city pavement and then, on another day, to do the same in a small village. When he appeared to collapse and then lay motionless on the pavement in a city centre, he was repeatedly ignored by the stressed urbanites as they hurried about their business. Some looked away and pretended not to see him. Some glanced at his body and then walked around him, offering no help to his seemingly stricken form. Dozens of citizens passed him in this way before, after about five minutes, someone paused, bent down and offered help.

In the village, in stark contrast, there were immediate offers of help, as soon as the fallen figure was spotted. In order to be sure that these were typical reactions, the falling down routine was repeated all over the village. Every time there was the same, unhesitating response. On the last occasion, an old lady emerged from her cottage to offer help. With a beaming smile, she bent over the prostrate figure and said: 'Oh, you are the man who keeps collapsing. Do come in a have a cup of tea.'

This comment revealed that the villagers were not merely individually helpful, but that word had got round the community that a visitor was in trouble and needed assistance. This is the type of cooperative behaviour that is a fundamental feature of human nature and which operates efficiently, even today, providing we are still living in small groups like our ancient ancestors.

GENETIC HAPPINESS
The Relative

Within the realm of tribal cooperation there is a special source of high-intensity happiness: the joys of the reproductive 'family unit'. The urge to reproduce one's own kind is such a powerful biological imperative that success in this endeavour brings moments of great 'genetic happiness'. Each phase of the process – falling in love, pair-bonding, giving birth and successfully rearing the offspring – has the potential to create great waves of primeval happiness. If all goes well, these landmark moments create such a powerful emotional response that they result in vivid memory traces that last a lifetime. So potent are they that, sadly, when they go wrong, the mental scars can also last for a lifetime.

The love for a partner or a child exceeds anything seen in ordinary tribal friendships because of the genetic factor involved. The essence of reproduction is the passing on of genetic material to future generations, and even for those who do not believe in the religious version of the afterlife, there is the reassuring thought that their offspring will at least provide them with a genetic immortality.

'Falling in love' is a powerful emotional experience in our species and one that sets us apart from other monkeys and apes. I have already mentioned that, when our ancient ancestors adopted the lifestyle of hunter-gatherers, the physical separation of the hunting males and the food-gathering females created new problems that were unknown to other primate societies. The males had to want to return to the human settlement with the spoils of the hunt, and their females had to want to be there when they did so. The evolution of a powerful bond of attachment between individual males and females therefore helped to ensure that the new, uniquely human division of labour worked efficiently.

But there was more to 'falling in love' than this. The setting up of pair-bonds also had the effect of doubling the parental care of the offspring. A typical monkey baby is reared solely by its mother. A human baby, with its greatly extended childhood, is reared by it mother and its father. By offering its growing infants paternal love in addition to maternal love, the human species was able to give itself a major survival boost and provide the young with much greater protection. This gave the greatly enlarged human brain time to become fully 'programmed' with experiences before sexual maturity and adulthood arrived on the scene.

All this was a vital part of the human evolutionary success story and results in a major new source of human happiness that is lacking in other monkeys and apes: the delirious happiness of the young lovers during the intense process of pair-formation. Although love and sex are intimately related, it is clear that the joy of love and the joy of sex are two distinct sensations. It is possible to fall in love without having sex and to have sex without falling in love. The sensual happiness of loveless sex can be powerful enough, and the more ethereal pleasures of platonic love have been well-documented, but when the two are combined, the result, in terms of emotional intensity, can be explosive and can provide what are probably the most acute moments of happiness known to human beings.

Equipping our species with this extreme form of passionate experience has gone a long way to help in ensuring the strength of the parental emotions that follow naturally upon the heels of sexual love. When the pair-bonded couple produce their first baby, there is, again, a welling-up of powerful loving emotion. Both the father and the mother are genetically programmed to respond strongly to the arrival of a new offspring and to protect and nurture it. This is yet another major source of genetic happiness.

The unusual longevity of our species – greater than that of any other kind of primate – appears to have evolved, in part, as a grandparental support system. To understand the need for this, it has to be remembered that, uniquely, the human female produces a 'serial litter'. Other primate females produce a baby, rear it to independence, and then start over again with the parental cycle. The short childhood of their offspring makes this feasible. But with human offspring, a whole decade of childhood has been added to the life cycle, allowing for the programming of the giant 'computer in the skull', and this creates a special breeding problem for our species.

If human females waited for their first offspring to become independent before starting to produce a second one, this would drastically slow down the reproductive cycle. The solution, during the course of evolution, was to overlap the dependent offspring. As a result, the human female must face the task of rearing a whole family of young, of varying ages but all in a state of prolonged dependency.

This creates a maternal burden so heavy that she needs all the help she can get. The solution is the 'extended family' and the addition, not only of a protective father, but also of caring grandparents. This important grandparental role (so often weakened by modern urban conditions) creates yet another potential source of great genetic happiness: the joy of caring for one's grandchildren.

SENSUAL HAPPINESS
The Hedonist

Many people, when asked what brings them a moment of happiness, mention the savouring of a delicious meal, a sexual experience, or some other pleasure of the flesh. Dr. Johnson said that happiness was a good tavern. The creed of the hedonist is that we should all give ourselves up to these primary biological pleasures as often and as strongly as possible.

The most intense form of sensual happiness is, without question, the orgasm. No species can survive without a massive inbuilt reward for the key moment of reproduction. Among our relatives, the monkeys and apes, the orgasm is confined to the males, but in humans it occurs in the females as well, and this difference requires an explanation.

In typical monkeys and apes, the female comes into heat at the time of ovulation and this involves the development of a sexual swelling around her genitals. This is visually conspicuous and excites the males who try to mount her and copulate with her. When the male ejaculates (usually after only a few seconds of mating) he reaches his momentary peak of sexual happiness and wanders off. The female reaches no such climax and remains sexually aroused until the period of heat passes and her sexual swelling goes down. Now she will lose her sexual appetite and will cease to be sexually attractive until her next swelling occurs, in a month's time, assuming she has not become pregnant.

With humans, a new mating system has evolved. The females do not develop any sexual swellings and give no indication that they are ovulating. Strangely, they hide this vital moment from their males. Furthermore, they remain sexually attractive and retain a strong sexual appetite at times when they are not ovulating. They are capable of sexual arousal even when they are menstruating or are pregnant. At such times, the mating acts are, of course, doomed to be non-procreative. They must therefore have some other function. It seems that, during the course of human evolution, female sexuality has been co-opted as part of a pair-bonding process; it has literally become lovemaking. As already mentioned, typical monkeys and apes do not form breeding pairs, but typical human beings do, and the extended sexual activity appears to have become part of the emotional cement that helps to hold the couple together.

While the male is rewarded by being able to have sex when his female is not ovulating, the female is rewarded by being able to experience a climactic orgasm as intense as that of the male. So, for the human species, the potential for sexual happiness has been greatly increased at a biological level. It has also been further heightened by cultural embellishments, as simple sexual activity becomes refined into advanced and prolonged forms of eroticism. For hundreds of years there are have been instruction manuals available that describe the many postures, movements and caresses that can be explored to prolong and intensify the moments of human sexual happiness. From the *Kama Sutra* of third-century India to the Kinsey reports and *The Joy of Sex* of the modern western world, and countless works of sexual fiction from all ages, there has always been a rich source of information for anyone wishing to increase their sexual pleasures. Attempts to suppress such information have merely driven it underground, taking it from the elegantly erotic to the crudely pornographic. As a source of intense human happiness, sexual activity is far too basic to be restricted for very long.

It is the same with food and drink. Obtaining food when you are starving or water when you are dying of thirst must provide moments of happiness as intense as anything else imaginable. Fortunately, most of us never reach such extremes, but we can still enjoy the daily pleasures of the table.

Even if we are not particularly hungry or thirsty, we continue to eat and drink – such is the intensity of this type of carnal activity. Just as we have enlarged our basic reproductive activities to develop an advanced world of human eroticism, so have we embellished basic feeding and drinking activities to develop the advanced world of the gourmet and the imbiber.

For thousands of years, the flavours of our foods and our drinks have been artificially improved in a hundred different ways. Eating basic, unimproved, wild foods of the kind enjoyed by our ancient ancestors for a million years is now comparatively rare. With some African tribes, it is still possible today to watch the intense happiness of a group of hunters who, immediately following a kill, proceed to drink the prey's hot blood direct from its fallen body. On a much wider scale, it is also possible to observe the joy of oyster-eaters as they devour their shellfish alive. But these primitive forms of eating are today the exception rather than the rule. Most meat is taken from modified, domestic animals and most botanical food is obtained from improved, domestic forms of plants.

Food preparation has also been developed to a point where most items on the menu have been transformed in some way as part of a global movement towards intensifying the happiness of the primeval activity of eating. The cooking of food started back in the Old Stone Age, but at that stage was confined to the roasting of meat. Then, in the New Stone Age, about ten thousand years ago, boiling and grinding were added to our culinary repertoire. Our first 'improved foods', after roasted meat, were such things as porridge, biscuits and cakes. By the Iron Age, about three thousand years ago, an early Egyptian would have had the choice of over thirty different kinds of bread and cakes, and more than a dozen different vegetables. As cities grew, ancient cuisine was increasingly elaborate and great feasts became a source of gourmet happiness on a grand scale.

The preparation of alcoholic drinks is also ancient. The earliest records of cultivated grapevines date from around 6000 BC in the Middle East. And the Sumerians in the fourth millennium BC enjoyed as many as nineteen different kinds of beer. Strong spirits appeared later, coming of age about one thousand years ago, usually concocted by bored monks to relieve the tedium of their celibate, monastic existence. By the thirteenth century AD, it was already being recorded that the search for happiness in the bottom of a glass was creating a 'serious social problem'.

Over the centuries, other pleasures of the flesh have included various forms of bathing, oiling and massaging, and improved resting equipment that offered greater comfort to the weary. The oldest known bathtub, found on the island of Crete in the Minoan palace at Knossos, is thirty-six hundred years old. It was placed in a beautifully decorated, en-suite bathroom in the queen's apartments, and clearly provided her with a sensual luxury appropriate for her rank. In ancient Greece, exhausted travellers were often greeted with the delights of a hot bath accompanied by a sensuous rubbing down in perfumed oils by handmaidens. Communal bathing was popular in ancient Rome, and Turkish baths are still with us to this day.

In modern times, the sensual pampering of the human body has grown into a major industry, and many people find it a source of happiness so relaxing that it borders on the tranquil (*see* page 92).

CEREBRAL HAPPINESS
The Intellectual

Because the human brain has become so enlarged during the course of evolution, it has now reached the stage where it can create a feeling of happiness simply by playing games with itself. These games vary from the most trivial – card games and computer games – to the most profound: artistic creativity and scientific research. There are those who will argue that all such activities have an ulterior motive (winning a contest, making money or advancing one's career), but these are by-products. The essence of all these preoccupations is that they exercise the brain and involve complex thought processes that are, at base, an end in themselves.

Scientific research is a good example. To outsiders, this is always seen as a carefully planned procedure with laudable end-goals that will benefit mankind.

In reality, as any scientist will admit when pressed, the real thrill of research is playing with complicated mental puzzles. 'Benefiting mankind' is usually only woven into the research plans in order to facilitate a research grant. The true pleasure in carrying out research lies in the intellectual pleasure of asking new questions and finding new answers. The moments of happiness arrive, often unexpectedly, when something novel is discovered. This may or may not benefit mankind. If it does so, this is merely a bonus.

Frequently, the greatest discoveries of all come not from tightly orchestrated, applied research, but from seemingly playful, pure research, done for its own sake. Government grant-giving bodies are not always fully aware of this, with the result that they end up sponsoring many minor advances, while missing out on the major ones. Scientists are at their best when they are left to their own devices, finding moments of intense cerebral happiness as they play mind-games with their material and, willy-nilly, change our world dramatically in the process.

Again, with artistic creativity, the greatest achievements are not made in the area of slickly produced commercial art, but in the often ramshackle world of fine art. Great artists do not think about how much a painting will sell for, or how much it will please other people. They work primarily for themselves, often in the certain knowledge that what they are doing will not be popular or even saleable.

In his entire life, Van Gogh sold only one picture, yet today his works have fetched the highest prices at auction of any artist in the history of the world. He was not driven by ulterior motives, but by the passionate mind-games he was playing with himself. With each new canvas, he set out to create images that satisfied him and gave him a massive burst of cerebral happiness at the moment of successful completion. Sadly, many artists demand so much of themselves that they find such moments of intense joy extremely rare. But when they do occur, they make all the labour and deprivation worthwhile.

For those who enjoy the results of these artistic labours, there is today an enormous range of possibilities for experiencing moments of intense aesthetic happiness. With countless museums, exhibitions and art publications available to us, we have no excuse if we allow this form of cerebral pleasure to pass us by. The same is true of other art forms. Modern recording techniques, for example, have advanced to such a state that we could, if we wished, enjoy the abstract sound patterns that we refer to as music, from waking to sleeping every day.

At the less intense level of popular indoor games, the brain sets itself tasks that it will find difficult, but not impossible. The pressure is off in such cases because the games have no meaning outside their special sphere. Interestingly, this type of activity is far from being a modern phenomenon. We know from archaeology that board-games of various kinds have been around for literally thousands of years. In hunter-gatherer societies in Africa, when the men returned from the hunt, they passed a great deal of their spare time playing mathematical games involving counting and strategy, often using little more than pebbles and holes scooped in the ground. This prehistoric pastime spread all over Africa, and stone-carved examples have been found in Egyptian temples dating from 1400 BC. Today it is often played on beautifully carved, wooden boards. It is popular in literally hundreds of different tribes and has almost as many native names, but it is more popularly known as Mancala.

Other ancient board-games include the amazingly complicated Game of Twenty Squares, discovered in the royal tombs at Ur and dating from 2500 BC, and Senet, the forerunner of backgammon, known from 2400 BC. The difficult Japanese game called Go was originally invented by the Chinese emperor Shun, who lived between 2255 and 2206 BC, and who devised it specifically to improve the intelligence of his son. The still-popular game of draughts, or checkers, originates from Egypt and dates from 1600 BC.

Most famous of all the mind-games played on a board is undoubtedly chess, and over the years it has exercised some of the most brilliant human brains. It has been played for at least nineteen centuries; the oldest-known chessmen, carved from ivory, and dating from the second century AD, were recently found in Russia. Although it was originally designed to demonstrate military strategy (it was the Arab battle cry *Shah Mat*, meaning 'The King is Dead' that gave us the word 'checkmate'), it has long since become a game of pure cerebral activity, with no ulterior motive or practical application. The moments of intense happiness involved – as when making a clever, unexpected move, for example – have no value whatever beyond the game itself.

Much the same is true with other indoor games, such as backgammon (eleventh century), poker (sixteenth century), whist (sixteenth century), cribbage (seventeenth century), bridge (a nineteenth-century refinement of whist), ludo (introduced in the nineteenth century as a westernized version of the ancient Indian game of pachisi), Scrabble (introduced in 1931), and a host of others. Some people see all of these as a complete waste of time because they do not lead anywhere. But they are not supposed to do so. They are merely devices that allow the players to experience moments of intense cerebral happiness, when games are played well. For the purists, adding high stakes to the proceedings simply destroys the quality of the games.

Like indoor games, puzzles provide huge opportunities for trivial forms of cerebral happiness. These range from quizzes and brain-teasers to such things as the Rubik's Cube (invented in 1979) and crossword puzzles (invented in 1913). Completing *The Times* crossword each day has become an important minor source of happiness for thousands of people, even though they are fully aware that it does not make them winners in a contest, brings them no financial reward, and has no ultimate, long-term target. It is purely an end in itself, an exercise for the brain, with the puzzler pitting his or her wits against the deviser of the crossword.

RHYTHMIC HAPPINESS
The Dancer

There is a special kind of happiness associated with intensely rhythmic activities. We see this in music, dancing, singing, aerobics, gymnastics, athletics and even in such odd activities as revivalist religious celebrations, synchronized swimming, dervish whirling, voodoo possession rituals, and military marching. Wherever a human activity involves a 'beat', there is the potential for finding oneself carried off into a strangely vertiginous sense of euphoria. All intellectual control is abandoned and given over to the tyranny of the beat. There is a sudden surge of pleasure as the rhythm takes hold and all else is momentarily forgotten. Sharing this with others helps to intensify the experience.

The fans at the pop concert, with their arms in the air, swaying together from side to side; the football fans chanting and clapping in synchrony in support of their team; the goose-stepping soldiers on ceremonial duty; the bible-belt faithful swinging back and forth as they pray together; the health fanatics prancing together aerobically in the gymnasium in search of the 'burn': all experience a unique kind of rhythmic happiness that has a special quality they find hard to define. Essentially it has to do with giving oneself up to a primitive physical sensation in which the brain switches off the higher centres for a while (and with that switching-off, temporarily removes all the usual cares and worries of the day) and allows the muscles of the body to enjoy a long series of evenly repeated actions.

Of course, our very lives are rhythmically controlled: by our heartbeat and breathing rate. As babies we were comforted by being rocked back and forth in our cradles or in our parents' arms. It follows that if, as adults, we start to move our whole bodies in the same way, we are tapping into something truly primeval.

Some people manage to go through their whole lives without ever giving themselves over to this particular kind of happiness. They are the ones who cannot face the thought of even briefly abandoning their intellectual controls and 'letting go'. For them, the very concept of rhythmic happiness will be alien to their thinking. Even if they attend a musical concert it will be to listen to music that excites the higher centres of their brains: orchestral music without a steady beat and with complex variations in speed and pattern.

By contrast, the simpler folk-music of every tribal gathering, dance hall, or pop concert will, despite its thematic variations, rely heavily on imposing a set rhythm on both its performers and its listeners. In the most extreme form, found at 'rave' concerts, there is little thematic variation left, the music having been simplified to little more than a deafening, thumping beat. Under its insistent bombardment, the ravers sway and gyrate in a state that is as far removed from intellectual debate as it is possible to get. This is rhythmic happiness at its most pure.

Underlying this type of happiness is a physiological reaction of the body involving an increase in the release of endorphins. These are the body's natural painkillers, chemically related to morphine, (the word 'endorphin' is a contraction of 'endogenous morphine', meaning 'the body's natural morphine'), and their impact is to create a mood of euphoric well-being. Their activation improves dramatically as the body reaches its highest state of intense rhythmic expression, and this fact has been used to explain the existence of what is called 'the runner's high' – and also why some exercise-fanatics become so addicted to their energetic work-out regimes.

Research at the Georgia Institute of Technology in America has, however, suggested that a different chemical, also released by energetic rhythmic activities, is the key factor involved in creating 'the runner's high'. It is a recently discovered pain regulator called 'anandamide' (a term derived from the Sanskrit word meaning 'internal bliss'), and it has been pointed out that this substance is closely related to the active ingredient in cannabis.

The researchers therefore suggest that the happiness 'high' of the exercise fanatic and the happiness 'high' of the cannabis smoker are very similar.

Anticipating, perhaps with some alarm, that this discovery might mean that warnings against cannabis-use might now also have to be applied to energetic exercise regimes, they have been quick to issue a denial of this, stating:

> In exercise, there is a reason why the [anandamide] system is activated. One has to deal with a physical stressor and the [anandamide] system fulfills its purpose. Smoking marijuana is a different story. This is an unnatural abuse of the system, not intended to be used this way by evolution.

PAINFUL HAPPINESS
The Masochist

For any well-balanced, cheerful individual, this is the most difficult form of happiness to comprehend. How can anyone develop a state of mind that equates pain with pleasure? Evolution has endowed us with an emergency alarm system that sends pain signals to the brain as a warning that we are physically or mentally at risk. As children, we quickly learn to avoid touching something that is very hot, or exposing ourselves to situations that cause mental agony. This is a vital self-protection system that helps us to escape injury or distress. It is the most basic of all survival systems and one can see it operating even among the lowest forms of animal life. And yet, despite this, some strange human adults turn this system on its head and seek out pain as a means to achieving a state of ecstatic pleasure. In bizarre sado-masochistic rituals, they have themselves tied up and beaten, or physically tormented in other ways. This is a rare form of happiness, but for those involved it means a great deal, and cannot be ignored.

At a lower level of intensity, there is the mental masochism of the puritan and the prude. For these individuals, happiness comes in the form of self-denial. They develop a mental outlook that sees any form of indulgence as disgusting and wicked. If eating chocolate or ice-cream provides a minor form of pleasure, then they must be avoided at all costs. Major pleasures, such as erotic sex and feasting are strictly forbidden. Alcohol makes people far too happy, so it must be banned.

This is the masochistic happiness of the anti-hedonist. The more frugal, austere and prohibitive life can be made, the greater their happiness. In origin, their attitude is usually born of the early discovery that other people are having fun and they are not. It they cannot have fun, then being funless must somehow be converted into an attractive proposition. They start to deny themselves pleasures and to enjoy the act of denial as a form of spiritual superiority. Each new renouncement of a personal pleasure becomes accompanied by a pang of smugly chaste happiness. This process, once begun, can easily escalate to reach levels of self-flagellation and self-restraint that reduce the life of the mental masochist to a stunted, bleak experience that is a travesty of human existence.

What these puritanical fanatics do to their own lives is their own choice and their own misfortune, but it does not usually stop there. All too often, the extreme abstinence of the anti-hedonist is not confined to his or her own behaviour. Attempts are eventually made to impose it on everyone else as well, and at this point it becomes a pernicious intrusion into the life of society at large. The American journalist, H. L. Mencken, summed this up well when he said, 'There is only one honest impulse at the bottom of Puritanism, and that is the impulse to punish the man with a superior capacity for happiness.'

When Puritanism starts to take hold of a whole country, in no time at all there is a growing tyranny of prohibited activities. Human pleasures become painted as debauched, dissolute, extravagant excesses. Public figures and social leaders, fearful of being accused of harbouring wayward or salacious preferences, feel the need to give (secretly reluctant) support to the waves of puritanical rebellion that they see spreading around them. Before long, the entire culture has become infected and the anti-hedonists have won. Their special form of masochistic happiness has taken hold. A classic example of this in recent years was the rise of the Taliban in Afghanistan, where even the commonplace sources of daily happiness such as listening to music, watching television, dancing, or visiting the cinema were banned.

Finding fulfilment in imposing misery on others in this way sounds, superficially, rather like sadism, but this is not the case. The primary motive of the prohibitors is not to take pleasure in hurting others, but rather to infect them with the same brand of masochistic happiness that they themselves have come to enjoy. They want to share their self-denial pleasures with everyone else.

Mental masochists come in several forms. There are the health fanatics, the diet-slaves, the teetotallers, the vegans, the anti-smokers and the celibates, each with his or her own special focus of interest. And there are others with a more general interest in pursuing the frugal way of life in all its aspects.

Of course, there is often a small price to pay for indulging in the hedonistic pleasures, but for the misery-makers this price becomes exaggerated a thousand times and they dwell on it endlessly. Something they prefer to ignore is that their claim to be generally healthier than unrepentant hedonists is not supported by the facts. A study of people who have managed to live for more than a century has revealed that a greater longevity is not guaranteed by any of the self-denial regimens. Indeed, the masochistic temperament that is needed for self-denial seems to shorten life rather than extend it.

Typically, the 100-plus individuals seem to be rather free-and-easy in their attitudes towards food, drink and other basic pleasures. Madame Jean Calment, the Frenchwoman who was the oldest person ever to have lived, was drinking cheap booze, smoking cigarettes and dining on foie gras and Provençal stew throughout her long life. When she reached the age of 117, an attempt was made to stop her drinking port and smoking, but she did her best to foil her doctors and was still indulging herself whenever she got the chance, right up to her death at the age of 122.

To be fair, Madame Calment was never excessive in her pursuit of pleasure. Obviously, if you eat, drink or smoke too much, your health will suffer. But equally, if you become obsessively disciplined in your self-denial, you will also run health risks. The ideal solution is moderation, rather than excess or denial.

Whatever vegans may claim, their diet is in reality inferior to that of people who enjoy a more varied diet. Human beings did not evolve as vegetarians — they succeeded because they mixed meat and vegetable elements to create a healthy, omnivorous diet. Although the intentions may be good, to avoid meat is to deny human biology.

Although heavy smoking is clearly a killer, the occasional cigarette or after-dinner cigar does not appear to do any harm. Again, heavy drinking is also a killer, but a small amount of alcohol each day may be beneficial.

So, in the end, the exaggerated self-restraint that provides happiness based on mental masochism appears to be far less rewarding that its practitioners would have you believe. Theirs is a mean-spirited, priggish form of happiness based on a lifestyle that, in the long run, does more harm than good.

Finally, one extreme form of Painful Happiness that sadly cannot be ignored today is the suicidal happiness of the terrorist. This is the ultimate form of self-inflicted pain, where the religious fanatic blows himself (or herself) to bits in order to kill and maim members of the enemy society.

This act is carried out in a state of bliss, and the moment of pressing the button is accompanied by a surge of unimaginable happiness, because the brainwashed bomber has been indoctrinated with the idea that to die in this way is the path to holy martyrdom that will ensure a swift passage to a heavenly state of eternal happiness in the afterlife.

The religious concept of the afterlife has a lot to answer for.

DANGEROUS HAPPINESS
The Risk-Taker

Deliberate, voluntary risk-taking is a source of happiness for certain individuals who find life lacking in rash challenges. As already explained, the primeval hunting existence turned our ancient ancestors into regular risk-takers, ready to accept the dangers of pursuing large prey. We became brave in a way that was unknown to tree-dwelling monkeys. Many people today are perfectly content to avoid acts of bravery and to enjoy a quiet life that is as risk-free as possible, but some find this too tame an existence and crave the excitements of surviving self-imposed hazards. The happiness comes, of course, not in facing the challenge, but in successfully overcoming it. The moment of safety following the risk is the time when a surge of primeval happiness courses through the veins.

There are two widely popular forms of risk-taking today: gambling and extreme sports. Gambling puts the bank balance at risk, but does not damage the risk-taker's body. A big win at the roulette table, the poker game, the national lottery, the bingo parlour, the tombola, or the races produces such a massive 'high' for the inveterate gambler that all the 'lows' are momentarily forgotten. Such is the impact of this surge of happiness that it reinforces the gambling urge, even if the total winnings from the few 'highs' are outweighed ten times by the total deficit from the many 'lows'.

With extreme sports, the position is rather different. A single 'low' here can cost the risk-taker his or her life, and the game is over for good. 'Nanny' governments try to protect people from their own, self-imposed follies by outlawing various dangerous sports, but this fails to stop the more adventurous ones. Not for them the approved thrills of fairground fun and big-dipper riding, or, more seriously, mountain-climbing and skiing. For them, illegality is almost a required condition of an extreme sport for it to provide the ultimate joy of danger-survival. Mountaineering up the sides of tall buildings, for example, or parachuting from the tops of them, are both popular among the risk-addicted minority, even though these activities may incur the wrath of the authorities.

Among the most dangerous of all the new extreme sports are those that involve riding on the outside of underground railway carriages. In New York this is known as subway-surfing and in London as Tube-surfing. Young men cling on to the tops or backs of carriages and try to avoid being thrown off as the trains speed along. They do not always succeed, with lethal results.

In recent years there has been an amazing proliferation in danger-sports, and this has resulted in the establishment of organizations such as the Dangerous Sports Club and the Extreme Sports Association. To give some idea of just how varied the quest for this type of human happiness has become, here is a list of just a few of the sports involved. Some are well-established and legally permitted, others are not: base-jumping, body-boarding, bridge-jumping, bungee-jumping, catapulting, cave-diving, dirt-boarding, hang-gliding, kite-boarding, kite-surfing, land-sailing, Le Parkour, microlighting, mountain-boarding, paragliding, sand-boarding, ski-boarding, sky-diving, sky-surfing, snow-boarding, steep-skiing, street luge, stunt pogo, surfboarding, wake-boarding, whitewater rafting, wing-walking, and wingsuit sky-flying.

The exponents of these sports are clear about their motivations. They are not seeking fame or fortune, like mainstream sportsmen. Instead they have as their objective little more than the excitement of avoiding the dangers they have imposed on themselves. To perform one of their exploits and come out unscathed at the end of it is enough, and they have mottos such as 'The key to happiness is freedom, and the key to freedom is courage' and 'Measure life by the things that take your breath away – not by the number of breaths you take.' They are scathing about those who are too scared to take part in their activities, advising 'To avoid personal injury, carefully follow these instructions: stay inside, stay in bed, don't fall out of the bed, do nothing but sleep.'

It seems inevitable that the more society struggles to cotton-wool its inhabitants, the more seeking of 'dangerous happiness' we shall see. As we become increasingly cosseted in a seat-belted, speed-limited world, there will always be those who will rebel by exposing themselves to the exhilaration of life-threatening pastimes. This is yet another way in which the ghost of the courageous, primeval hunter haunts us still.

SELECTIVE HAPPINESS
The Hysteric

This is happiness that depends on ignoring the horrors of life all around one. People who suffer from depression believe that they are the only ones who are seeing the world in its true light and that happy people are simply missing – or deliberately ignoring – the terrible problems and pains of existence. They cannot understand how anyone can ever enjoy a moment's happiness when there are starving millions, torture prisons, animal experiments, polluted environments or whatever particular disaster area they are most concerned with. This has led several people to define happiness in most uncomplimentary terms. No less a person than Einstein referred to happiness as 'the ideal of the pigsty'. And when you look at photographs of the great sad face of the old genius, you can see that he wasn't exactly a laugh a minute. He knew too much to be happy and was apparently incapable of switching off that great burden of knowledge, even for a brief moment. Others who have similar views have defined happiness as hysterical oblivion, innocence, unintelligence and the serenity of fools.

There is an upside and a downside to hysteric happiness. The upside is that those exhibiting the hysteric personality are usually more fun to be with. The downside is that they can create chaos for those around them. Because they refuse to recognize the problems that life throws at them, they are able to exist is a state of blissful cheerfulness. The old saying about Nero fiddling while Rome burned comes to mind. Hysterics are capable of having a good time even when disaster is all around them. Eventually, of course, it will catch up with them, but for the moment, they can manage to ignore it. If they happen to have enough talent, they may be forgiven for ignoring the chaos, but eventually it comes home to roost.

An elderly Dutch artist I once knew, who lived and painted in a small cottage in the middle of a forest, once said to me, 'If I did everything I had to do, I would never get anything done.' What he meant was that if he kept his studio dusted and tidy, dealt efficiently with his correspondence, and paid attention to all the other daily trivia that most people consider essential to their well-being, he would never have the time or energy to sit at his easel painting his pictures. His style of painting was difficult and demanding and took many hours of intense concentration. If he had not ignored the other aspects of his daily life, his important work would have suffered.

But he was really only a semi-hysteric, because he was aware of the fact that he was ignoring matters that he considered to be trivia. A full-bloodied hysteric is not even aware of *what* he is ignoring; he manages to blot it out completely. The semi-hysteric, while gaining a powerful happiness from devoting himself to his rewarding work, nevertheless has a faint worry at the back of his mind about all the commonplace, humdrum duties he really ought to be performing, like everyone else, but is willfully ignoring in order to achieve his special goal.

The artist Francis Bacon was another example of someone who was capable of ignoring the ordinary in his pursuit of the extraordinary. At the time, late in his life, when his paintings were selling for several million pounds each, he was still occupying a small bed-sitting room next to his cramped studio. His bath was in his tiny kitchen and the rooms were lit by naked light-bulbs. At the celebrations for his eightieth birthday, he was given bouquets of flowers by well-wishers, but commented wryly, 'How ridiculous – I am not the sort of person who has vases.' Even his laundry had to be organized for him by his art gallery. For many creative people, there is a stubborn refusal to waste time on everyday matters, and some, like Bacon, show a remarkable ability to blot out anything that distracts them.

TRANQUIL HAPPINESS
The Meditator

This is the form of happiness that is obtained by contemplation and isolation from the cares of the world. The meditator's goal is to find an inner peace. It is related to the last category, but here there is a deliberate philosophical or religious shutting out of the rest of the world and a turning in on oneself, rather than a temporary side-stepping of worldly problems.

To many people, this type of happiness appears out of tune with true human nature. If human beings are, by their very nature, active, striving, exploratory individuals, full of curiosity and energy, the idea that higher states of consciousness can be obtained by letting the mind go blank is hard to understand from an evolutionary point of view. To typically energetic individuals, it seems that, even if the meditators are having a happy time inside their skulls, it is more likely that everyone else is having a much better time outside, where the action is.

The meditator's world may be pervaded by a sense of serenity, but this is too passive for most of us. There is no surge of emotion, no joyous elation: merely a quiet feeling of detachment. Within that detachment the meditators may well experience a sense of calm; for some people, this could be enormously rewarding, shutting them off from the cares of the world. But for me this amounts to an escape from reality rather than the discovery of a new, inner reality. For me, and I suspect for the majority of human beings, the world is too exciting a place to be shut off by an inward-looking philosophy.

To be fair, those who practice the pursuit of tranquil happiness as a serious preoccupation do have one advantage over the rest of us. If they have a sufficiently serene type of personality, one that allows them to switch off human curiosity for long periods of time, they can, if they are successful in their meditations, achieve a more prolonged state of happiness than the rest of us.

For the more typically active human beings, there are long stretches of anticipation with only occasional peaks of intense, surging happiness. But if meditators can truly find happiness in their inner searching, then they can, in theory, sustain this for much longer periods of time.

This is summed up well in the teachings of Buddha. The key to his philosophy is 'The Middle Way', which has been summarized as follows: 'Realizing both the self-destructiveness of those who deny their desires and the misery of those who follow their desires, the Buddha saw that there is a Middle Path, which is simply to lose one's desires.' In other words, the Buddha rejected the masochism of self-denial and the many inevitable disappointments of the out-and-out hedonist, and focused on the central zone between these two extremes. Viewed cynically, this is no more than a philosophy of compromise, of 'moderation in all things': the idea that one drink is good for you but twenty will rot your liver, etc., mild restraints instead of savage ones, or mild indulgences instead of debauched ones.

But that is not quite what the Buddha had in mind. He did not envisage The Middle Way as a moderate expression of desire, but rather of the loss of desire altogether. Rather than seeing the 'spectrum of desire' as a kind of scale, from totally inhibited to totally unleashed, he saw it instead as two opposed extremes between which there is a completely neutral point where no desire exists at all.

In that region, the mind finds peace and a state of Nirvana: a deep inner feeling of freedom and non-attachment. If this can bring tranquil happiness to the meditator, then in theory it has the advantage of being long-lasting rather than fleeting.

But whether it is possible to maintain, over a long period, the intensity of the surge of joy that the rest of us feel when we experience a peak moment of happiness, seems doubtful.

Tranquil happiness, it has to be said, sounds rather like the peace of death without any of the unpleasantness of dying.

DEVOUT HAPPINESS
The Believer

Deeply religious individuals claim to find a special kind of spiritual happiness when they experience their most reverent moments. In their quieter moods, their joy is akin to Tranquil Happiness, but in the fervour of their more passionate forms of worship, their happiness is much more active – and sometimes, even frenetic. When two million Muslim pilgrims reach Mecca or great throngs of Christians arrive at Lourdes, many of the participants experience a mood of religious ecstasy as they find themselves succumbing to feelings of overwhelming devotion to their respective deities. The mental bliss that suffuses them at these times requires some sort of explanation. The key element in this type of happiness is a total, blind faith in the tenets of a particular religion. If analytical thought, reasoned discussion, scientific debate, or even everyday common sense entered the scene, all would be lost. The deities involved must be almighty and all-powerful and their divine will must be obeyed at all times. A mass demonstration by the faithful followers of their devotion to their particular god-figure provides the best chance for experiencing the breathless passion of sacred or spiritual happiness.

Essentially what is happening in such cases is a switching on, at full blast, of long-lost infantile security, taken from those moments when a tiny child feels the great upwelling of happiness in the tender, loving embrace of a protective, all-powerful parent. This is something that we all secretly miss more and more as we grow up, and which we unconsciously continue to desire throughout our lives. Our matured egos and our adult responsibilities force us to suppress our desire to cry out for parental aid. But if we can find a new kind of symbolic super-parent, then we can once again enjoy a – now transformed – infantile role.

It is no accident therefore that, for thousands of years, the major deities have been known by parental titles such as The Mother Goddess, The Great Mother, The Earth Mother and, later on, after an unfortunate sex-change, as God the Father. This use of maternal and paternal names when referring to the deities has also been borrowed by some of their servants, as in the cases of (childless) Mother Superiors and (childless) priests who call themselves Fathers.

Any individual who is capable of momentarily suspending reason and of calling upon a supernatural super-parent for help may be able to find great happiness in this reversion to the trusting days of infancy, when the small child has complete faith in its biological parents and immediately runs to them whenever trouble strikes. Because the sacred super-parents are never present in the flesh, they are incapable of demonstrating any of the usual weaknesses of real human parents. They remain aloof, with their messages and their teachings passed on to their 'children' by astute middlemen who organize special ceremonial gatherings at which the faithful can work one another up into a shared passion of zealous devotion and divine frenzy.

The sensations experienced by these adult pseudo-children are real enough. The faithful do feel waves of joy pass through their bodies as they join together in honouring their god-figures, and the Devout Happiness of true believers cannot be overlooked. It underlines, yet again, the extent to which human evolution has been a neotenous trend, neoteny being the process by which an animal achieves adult status while retaining juvenile qualities. We are 'all God's children', it would seem — even when we are in our dotage.

NEGATIVE HAPPINESS
The Sufferer

Sigmund Freud favoured this approach, saying that 'Men try to obtain happiness by eliminating unhappiness'. It is a sad truth that being ecstatically happy is harder to sustain over long periods than being miserably unhappy. If an individual sustains a major tragedy in his (or her) life, such as the loss of a partner or the death of a child, he may find himself unable to regain a state of cheerfulness for a very long time. One eminent professor who felt responsible for the death of his son was observed to dress entirely in black for the rest of his life. In complete contrast, had he managed to snatch his son from the jaws of death, he would have felt a huge surge of happiness immediately afterwards, but his intense feeling of joy would not have lasted. In a similar way, the miserable aftermath of a bitter divorce can persist for years, whereas the uncontrollable outburst of happiness that accompanies the process of falling in love soon mellows and loses its emotional intensity. Time heals wounds slowly, but it dissipates happiness more swiftly.

It is for this reason that states of happiness are no more than punctuations in the life sentence we serve between our birth and our death. The best we can hope for is to have a pleasantly contented peace of mind for most of the time, interrupted only by peak moments of joyous intensity. For many people, however (especially the kind who ended up on Freud's couch), life is a great desert of mental anguish, with only an occasional oasis of pleasure. For them, as Freud pointed out, the quest for happiness is a search for answers to explain their anguish and eliminate it.

For others, who live in physical rather than mental pain, happiness comes in the shape of a bottle of painkillers. When it is time to take the pills again, the moment of relief from the prolonged pain is the classic moment of 'negative happiness'. For those who are healthy, feeling pain-free is the norm and is barely noticed. But for the chronically ill, moments of pain-relief bring them up to what is for them a peak of happiness. The sufferer's peak is the athlete's baseline.

For many people, who may not be in mental turmoil or physical agony, daily life may still fall far short of being a pleasant experience. They may be bored, lacking in direction, insecure, anxious or stressed, and their peak moments of happiness may be too trivial or too rare to compensate for their general feeling of malaise. For them, assuming they are incapable of re-structuring their lives, there are two special solutions. They can increase their happiness quotient (buying happiness to order) by resorting to either chemical happiness or fantasy happiness. In other words, they can escape into a world of chemical dreaming or day-dreaming — by using drugs or by escaping into a world of fiction.

CHEMICAL HAPPINESS
The Drug-Taker

Many people have sought a burst of happiness with the aid of a chemical substance of some kind. Drug-taking has been used for thousands of years as an extreme step in the quest for a happy state of mind. A rare use of narcotics can be looked upon as no more than a risky exploration of sensory responses – no more than a satisfying of human curiosity. Regular use, however, looks more like a failure to find daily life sufficiently stimulating. Or it may be that personal misery and internal turmoil can create such an overriding feeling of depression or despair that the only hope of finding release from reality is to escape into a chemically controlled world of new and intense sensation. For such troubled people, only a narcotic-induced state can shut off the pain long enough for them to experience brief moments of euphoria and the welling up of a powerful emotional state of happiness.

Unfortunately, there is a heavy price to pay for this joyful escape when serious addiction (using hard drugs) takes hold. The return to harsh reality, when the effects of the drug wear off, is so distressing that another dose is soon sought, and another and another. Other aspects of daily life become ignored, health suffers, and a downward spiral of drug dependency begins to destroy the addict's existence. Brief moments of chemical happiness are still experienced, of course, with each new (and often stronger) dose, but these moments are outweighed by the unhappiness that follows.

To be fair, there are many so-called 'soft drugs' that do provide moments of happiness without causing too much after-damage. Tea, coffee, tobacco and alcohol are widely used on a global scale and are accepted by most cultures as legal forms of chemical happiness. Even with these, however, excessive use often leads to damaged health. The sad truth is that those individuals who are most likely to turn to chemical aids in the first place are also those who are most likely to become addicted in the second place. 'Moderation' is not a word that sits easily in any debate on drug-taking.

Despite desperate attempts by government authorities to suppress drug use, it still flourishes all over the world on a vast scale, and has done so for thousands of years. Today, there are many different kinds of 'happy pills' available from the pharmaceutical industry, but this is a comparatively new phenomenon. Older drugs, with a long social history can, by contrast, be traced back to the earliest civilizations and even beyond, into prehistoric times. Some of the most important ones are as follows.

For centuries, many Mexican Indian tribes, including the ancient Aztecs, have employed certain kinds of mushrooms as a source of hallucinogenic experiences. The most popular species is *Psilocybe mexicana*, a small, tawny-coloured mushroom that is found in marshy places. During religious ceremonies, the Indians eat about a dozen of these. At first there are unpleasant sensations, but these soon give way to an intensely happy state that lasts for a period of several hours, and during which the subject experiences an amazing range of extraordinary visions. This is followed by a period of mental and physical depression.

Related drugs with similar hallucinogenic effects are mescaline, obtained from the peyote cactus *Lophophora williamsii*, and LSD-25, usually referred to simply as 'acid', obtained from the rye fungus ergot, *Clavicaps purpurea*.

The mind-altering effects of LSD-25 were not discovered until 1943, when the Swiss chemist studying it accidentally ingested some. It became a popular recreational drug in the 1960s. Although it did not lead to physical addiction or withdrawal symptoms, like other powerful narcotics, it did have one major drawback: its impact was highly variable and unreliable. For one taker of LSD there might be a burst of intense happiness, while for another, taking an identical dose, there could be an experience of pure horror.

Among the Indian populations of the Andes, in South America, a widely used narcotic is obtained from the leaves of the coca plant, *Erythroxylon coca*. The leaves are picked, prepared and then chewed as a 'wad'. The active ingredient is cocaine, a refined form of which is also exported to other parts of the world where it has become a common recreational drug. It works directly on the central nervous system, and there is a surge of 'chemical happiness' that lasts for about half an hour. In moderation it apparently has few ill effects, but it is all too often used to excess, leading to insomnia, acute anxiety, confusion and, if snorted as a powder, the destruction of the interior of the nose.

An improved version of this drug, known as crack-cocaine (because of the cracking noise it makes when it is heated), has become popular in recent years.

Crack-cocaine users speak of experiencing a 'whole-body orgasm' and an intensity of happiness 'completely outside the normal range of human experience.' However, this exceptional 'high' is soon followed by a massive 'low', involving anxiety, depression, irritability, fatigue and paranoia.

Cannabis is the name of a hemp plant found originally in China and central Asia. *Cannabis sativa* produces a resin that is hallucinogenic. It is known by over two hundred names, the most commonly used being marijuana, bhang, hashish, ghanja, pot or grass. Its narcotic effects have been exploited for over five thousand years, and its use, although illegal in most places, is now worldwide.

Its impact is to create a sensation of indolent, dreamy, relaxed withdrawal from reality. It offers chemical happiness in the form of a light-headed euphoria in which sensory awareness is heightened, while the desire for action is decreased. Its main disadvantages are that it causes distorted depth-perception and impaired physical coordination.

This means that attempts to perform mechanically complex actions. such as driving a car or operating other kinds of machinery, are hazardous.

One of the oldest drugs known, opium has been is use since prehistoric times. A milky liquid is extracted from the opium poppy, *Papaver somniferum*, and dried to form a brown gum. When smoked, this gum quickly creates a state of chemical happiness by dramatically reducing anxiety (and pain if that is present) and by inducing a sensation of euphoria. Its downside is that it also causes both mental and physical impairment, apathy and sleep. The subject also experiences increasing tolerance to the drug, so that larger and larger doses have to be taken to obtain the desired effect. Furthermore, it is highly addictive, with severe withdrawal symptoms.

In 1803, morphine, an active ingredient of opium, was isolated and pressed into use medically as a powerful painkiller. Then, in 1897 in Germany, heroin was in turn derived from morphine. A white powder four times as strong as morphine, it eventually became the injected 'hard drug' of choice for addicts all over the world, superseding opium almost everywhere except in certain regions of Southeast Asia. Heroin initially rewards the drug-taker by creating an almost orgasmic reaction, followed by a mentally detached state of intense relaxation. Chemical happiness is achieved by switching off all fears, anxieties and feelings of depression. For individuals suffering a miserable or stressful existence, it clearly provides a massive relief. But there is a catch. Physical dependence soon develops and more and more of the drug is needed to satisfy the addict's craving. Without the drug there are now terrible withdrawal symptoms, and what started out as a quest for chemical pleasure is now a desperate struggle to avoid pain.

Summing up the question of chemical happiness, it must be concluded that there is nothing in favour of a lifestyle that sees the gaining of short-term happiness at the expense of long-term misery.

Because of this unbalanced equation, governments all over the world have made the taking of hard drugs illegal. It has to be said, however, that this step has been largely unsuccessful, and drug-trafficking remains to this day a vast global enterprise. (It has been estimated that, to give one example, no fewer than 300 million people today use cannabis in one form or another.)

An idealistic solution to this problem is one that sees modern society undergoing a major shift in emphasis — a shift which ensures that the human population as a whole is able to enjoy a challenging lifestyle that is well-tuned to the adventurous, enquiring spirit of human nature, so that everyone can get 'high' on daily life and have no need to resort to chemically induced 'improvements'. But in truth this is little more than naïve, wishful thinking. Despite all our other social advances, the global pursuit of chemical happiness remains a human problem that nobody has even begun to resolve.

FANTASY HAPPINESS
The Day-dreamer

Human beings have the unique ability to enjoy symbolic thought processes. Ever since our ancestors invented language, we have been able to make one thing stand for another. When we say 'tree' we immediately conjure up an image of a huge wooden shape rising up into the air, covered with leaves. The letters t, r, e, e and the sound they make when we say them bear no relation to the tall wooden object, and yet we are able to use the one to stand for the other. We take this so much for granted and yet it is the basis of one of our major sources of happiness in the modern world.

Because the development of verbal language fine-tuned us to the use of symbols, we are all now prepared to accept a fiction as if it were a fact. In ancient times, this began with day-dreaming and simple storytelling. As civilization advanced, it then developed into theatre and fictional writing, and eventually into radio, film and television. In all these cases, the human brain is capable of enjoying a great surge of happiness as some drama or comedy is played out in a way that appeals to us. We know that the events are not real, but we are able to suspend our sense of reality just long enough to enjoy them.

In our adult lives we spend countless happy hours reading novels, watching soap operas on TV, going to the movies, or achieving moments of personal glory in our day-dreams. Even as children we enjoy the thrills of fairy tales, cartoons and bedtime stories. The best fictional plots are designed specifically to give us those moments of peak happiness that are likely to be missing from much of our humdrum daily lives. When the villain dies, the lovers kiss, or the weakling triumphs, we are there in our imaginations, experiencing these intense moments at second hand.

As with chemical happiness, fantasy happiness is an escape from reality. Unlike chemical happiness, however, there is no direct health hazard. There is an indirect one, caused by the prolonged immobility of the fantasy addict – too much sitting (the couch potato syndrome) can lead to flabby muscles – but this is not inevitable. The novel-reader, the cinema goer and the television viewer are all free to take plenty of healthy exercise at other times of the day. The appetite for exciting fantasies cannot be blamed for laziness at other times.

Because they are so safe and so harmless, fantasies have become the major source of happiness in modern civilizations. With increasingly sophisticated technology, this trend looks set to grow and grow. It is easy to imagine a future where every living room has one huge plasma-wall on which is projected a perfect, three-dimensional image. Sitting in the comfort of our homes, we will all be able to enjoy repeated surges of intense happiness as our fantasies are brilliantly realized for us on this plasma wall.

The only downside of this inevitable development is the loss of real, active involvement in the dramas that we watch unfolding before us. But this loss is only temporary — while we are in our 'audience' mode — and still leaves us completely free to use other hours in the day enjoying reality rather than fantasy.

COMIC HAPPINESS
The Laugher

Whenever we laugh, something strange happens inside us. Just for a brief moment, we feel slightly healthier, as a surge of happiness passes through us. If a professional comedian makes us laugh again and again, the brief surge becomes a glow and we find ourselves still smiling as we make our way home.

We think of humour as a sophisticated, intellectual process, but there is something much more basic, more biological taking place as we laugh out loud. An important biochemical change is occurring in our systems. Endorphins are secreted inside us that have painkilling properties. Furthermore, recent research at the University of Wisconsin in the United

States has shown that 'the part of the brain that controls happy emotions can stimulate the immune system to work harder.' (Perhaps this explains why comedians Bob Hope and George Burns both lived to be 100.)

In an experiment at Indiana State University, one group of people was shown comedy films while a second group was made to watch solemn documentaries. Afterwards, tests revealed that those who had been enjoying the comedy films had the activity of their immune systems boosted by forty percent and had their stress hormones decreased.

So, if we are feeling under the weather, a few good jokes will biochemically make us feel a little better. This fact is now being exploited in the United States at certain cancer clinics. Fully costumed circus clowns are sent around the wards to make the patients laugh out loud, despite the pain and distress they are feeling as they lie in their beds. Employing comedians to entertain people who are dying of cancer may sound like a sick joke in more senses than one, but the truth is that such unorthodox procedures *do* actually work. They do not cure cancer, of course, but they make the pain much easier to bear.

If laughter causes happiness, both at the cerebral level and the biochemical level, then why don't we devote more of our time to being amused? That would seem, at first glance, to be an obvious way of increasing happiness in the world, but this is where the elusiveness of the mood we call happiness throws a massive spanner into the works.

For happiness refuses to be exploited. If we find something that makes us happy and we keep on repeating it, it soon palls. The intense joy of the first impact soon becomes mild pleasure and, finally, boredom. If joke-telling goes on, hour after hour and day after day, it soon starts to feel shallow and unreal. If, to give a trivial example of a different sort of experience, we feel a small pang of happiness when we taste the season's first strawberries, we will soon become jaded with them if we gorge on them at meal after meal. In no time at all we will be screaming that we never want to see another strawberry as long as we live.

What is it about jokes and funny stories that makes us laugh? To understand this, it helps to think back to the first time that laughter occurs in the life of an individual. With the human baby, crying is present from birth as a protection device, warning parents that something is wrong and needs urgent attention. Laughter, on the other hand, does not arrive until the third or fourth month of life, and appears to have evolved out of crying in a special way.

In several respects the two actions are very similar (and we often speak of 'laughing until we cried'). Like crying, laughing involves a tensing of the muscles, a wide opening of the mouth, a pulling back the lips, and exaggerated breathing. At high intensities both actions also include a reddening of the face and a watering of the eyes. But the accompanying vocalizations are strikingly different. Laughter is less rasping and not as high-pitched as crying; above all, the sounds are shorter and follow one another more rapidly. It is as though the long wail of the crying infant has become chopped up into little pieces, and at the same time has grown smoother and lower. So, although the facial contortions of crying and laughing are very similar, the accompanying vocal signals are easy to distinguish from one another.

The first sign that laughter is about to develop out of crying appears when the mother starts to play with her baby, lifting it up high, swinging it in the air, or going 'peek-a-boo'. Instead of crying with fear, the baby gurgles with pleasure. The reason that this does not happen until the infant is about four months old is because, before that age, it does not recognize its mother individually as a special person. The newborn reacts to all adults in much the same way. But the four-month-old baby has now become wary of strangers and is strongly imprinted on its mother, who it sees, at this stage, as its personal protector. So it feels safe with its mother and has a deep feeling of trust in her.

This means that, if she does something playful that startles her baby, the infant will be getting two signals at ones. One says, 'There is something nasty here' and makes the baby want to cry; but the other says, 'This is your mother, so all is well, there is nothing to fear.' The result is that the baby recognizes that something is frightening, but at the same times knows that it does not have to be taken seriously. The result is that it gives a little cry and a gurgle of maternal recognition, both at the same time. It is this that creates the 'gurgling cry' or 'segmented wail' that we call 'laughter'.

So, the birth of laughter in the first year if life comes with the recognition that 'I have experienced a danger that is not real.' It is a great relief to the baby to know that some apparently alarming actions are, in reality, perfectly safe and, as it grows up, it exploits this by running away and laughing happily when it is caught, or hiding and then laughing when it is discovered. In this way, playful versions of serious activities become a major source of infantile happiness.

We may play less when we become adult, but we never lose the capacity to enjoy 'safe fear', and this is what the professional comedian offers us. We know he is a comic and that nothing he says is to be taken seriously, so we know we are safe and, like the baby, we laugh and laugh. As we listen to his outrageous comments – most of which contain an attack on some form of authority – we enjoy the pleasure of confronting our fears in a completely secure context, and feel a surge of happiness coursing through our bodies.

Closely related to this is the pleasure children get from riding the big dipper at the fun-fair. They may scream as they plunge through the air, but they enjoy it because, once again, it is a 'safe fear', and they are nearly always convulsed with laughter as they step off at the end of the ride. In a similar way, older children enjoy horror films because, when they scream at the monster, they do so knowing full well that they are perfectly safe in their cinema seats.

ACCIDENTAL HAPPINESS
The Fortunate

Surprisingly this is the original definition of the word, because 'happiness' comes from 'happy' which comes from 'hap' which comes from the Old Norse and means 'good luck'. So, strictly speaking, if you are a linguistic purist, you should only feel happy when you have prospered from some lucky chance event, such as winning the lottery or finding a banknote in the street.

If you have worked hard for your moment of happiness, then it should be called something else. But this is too narrow a definition for use today. As a good example of accidental happiness, my personal favourite is the feeling you have when, after a long and tiring flight on a jumbo jet, it is your suitcase that comes up first on the carousel.

THE NATURE OF HAPPINESS

To sum up, my definition of happiness is the sudden surge of pleasure we feel when something gets better. The key to understanding happiness is that it only exists in an intense form when there has just been a dramatic improvement in some aspect of our lives. This 'moment of improvement' can be anything from a major experience, such as the arrival of a new baby, to something as trivial as a cold drink on a hot day.

Because it is linked to change, intense happiness is not a lasting sensation, but rather a fleeting one. When a sportsman is interviewed after winning an important trophy, and is asked how he feels, he often comments that 'It hasn't sunk in yet'. What he really means is that he is still in that emotional condition of acute happiness and that it has blotted out any kind of rational analysis of his achievement or what it might mean to his future career. He is still on the irrational, emotional 'high' that accompanies the mental state we call happiness. Only when he has calmed down will his analytical brain take over again and start to study his new situation. In the same way, the father who beams with delighted pride at the first sight of his new baby, fresh from his wife's womb, has all practical thoughts banished from his mind by the intense happiness that this key moment brings. Worries over dirty nappies and sleepless nights are totally absent at this point.

It is also clear that happiness comes in many forms and can be found in different contexts. For some, the achievement of an ambition brings a powerful moment of sometimes overwhelming happiness. For others, who set their sights too high, the inability to reach their lofty goals can easily condemn them to a life of self-imposed failure and disappointment. For the luckier ones, who are more modest in their goals, there can, by contrast, be many minor moments of happiness that, together, can add up to a great deal during a single lifetime.

The secret of increasing 'target happiness' lies in accepting that the human species is not suited to a life of trivial, repetitive behaviour that is lacking in serious challenges. Of course, we all have humdrum duties to perform day after day, but these must not be allowed to dominate our lives. We need to set aside part of our daily energy for more long-term pursuits, with a final, reachable goal. That goal must be realistic – not too high and not too low – and suited to our personal potential.

If our official work – our profession or employment – is varied and challenging, then we are the lucky ones who will need little more in the way of 'targets' to keep us happy. But if our daily work is a monotonous grind lacking in any kind of long-term achievement, or if we have been forced to go into a cosy but boring retirement, then we need to invent a spare-time challenge of some kind that will give us a personal target that suits our particular talents. Only in this way can we hope to enjoy the thrill of consummating a symbolic chase, and satisfying our primeval programming as tribal hunters.

For those who are unduly competitive, winning brings the greatest joy. Serious contests can easily result in damaging losses that may suppress happiness for a long period of time. The competitive urge that drives us on to find explosive moments of triumph can, however, be satisfied in a thousand minor ways, none of which need be taken too seriously. Modest sports and games can give us the opportunity of enjoying many moments of competitive happiness without suffering too much when we lose. When we win a game we can convince ourselves that it was extremely important, but when we lose we can equally convince ourselves that the outcome of the contest was not really of any great significance. This 'double-think' is hard to do in the case of major contests, but it can easily be carried off with minor ones and, in this way, we can greatly increase our sources of competitive happiness.

In complete opposition to this is the happiness gained from satisfying our primeval urge to cooperate with one another: the joy of being helpful and caring, especially to one's own offspring, but also to all members of one's 'tribe'. This is something that moralists usually take credit for, claiming that it is only their teachings that have instilled kindness in us. In reality, however, it is a basic element in human nature, for which we should thank our evolutionary past.

Enjoying the offering of love to a partner, a child or a grandchild is something that can bring with it great waves of intense happiness, but for those who have been unlucky in love or family matters, this form of joy may be conspicuously absent. In such cases, there are rewards to be had from offering one's love to a substitute of some kind. Pet animals such as dogs and cats fill this void for many people, and become substitute children with a great potential for bringing cooperative happiness to people who might otherwise suffer from an acute lack of love-giving. Because they are only substitutes, people who speak of their pets as their 'babies' or their 'children' are sometimes held up to ridicule, but this is thoughtless and unfair.

Other individuals who seek an outlet for their inborn, cooperative urges can find them in the region of many charities, when some special category of

human being – the sick, the deprived, the hungry –
is transmitting signals of helplessness that can easily
offer fulfilment for the cooperative urges of those
who are more fortunate. Sadly, there is no scarcity of
individuals, both human and animal, who are in need
of help, and it is easy enough, with a little effort, to
put oneself into a social context where cooperative
happiness can be increased.

Because we are animals, albeit unusually intelligent
ones, we still react strongly to the primary carnal
rewards of sex, food, drink and bodily comfort.
The fact that we do share these appetites with other
animals has meant that, foolishly, some people feel
a pang of guilt when indulging them. This stems in
part from centuries of religious teaching that has
denigrated animals and sought to elevate humans to
some imaginary, higher plane. Humans are said to
possess something called a 'soul', while it is insisted
that animals lack this magical ingredient. This now
deeply entrenched concept has given rise, not only
to centuries of animal abuse, but also to the idea
that anything we might share with other animals is

somehow suspect and inferior. Despite the obvious truth of Darwin's theory of evolution, the ghost of religion's imagined chasm between human and animal still haunts society. As a result there is, for many people, a lingering sense of unease whenever they find themselves uncontrollably enjoying some major (or even minor) carnal pleasure. The only way to increase carnal happiness is therefore to lay this ghost by examining the roots of carnal guilt and seeing it for what it is: an unnecessary fear kept alive by an outmoded form of primitive superstition.

For those individuals who are unable to free themselves from these ancient indoctrinations, an alternative source of happiness is to be found in the higher centres of their large brains in intellectual pursuits. These range from finding equations that will solve the riddles of the universe to playing simple mind-games, quizzes and puzzles.

For those whose daily work is not intellectually demanding, it is all too easy, in modern times with a hundred television channels to choose from, to sit back and let the brain go gently out of focus. For them, cerebral happiness can be given a kick-start by finding some sort of activity – no matter how trivial – that forces them to combine feats of memory with analytical thought processes. A regular indulgence in such activities can do for the brain what exercise and workout regimes do for the muscles.

Although they have been treated separately here, it is important to realize that these two, very different sources of great joy – sensual happiness and cerebral happiness – are not mutually exclusive. Human beings are in the fortunate position of being able to enjoy both to the full. The idea that sensual individuals are essentially debauched voluptuaries without a higher thought in their heads, or that cerebral individuals are inevitably nerdy swots who are scornful or ignorant of the more basic pleasures, is a popular myth. In reality, however, some of the greatest brains have also, in their private lives, proved to be exceptionally active in their pursuit of carnal pleasures.

Brilliant figures such as Balzac, Byron, Gauguin, Kennedy, Picasso, Stendhal, Toulouse-Lautrec, Van Gogh, Wells and Wilde were all carnally extremely active. Balzac, it is said, 'devoured his lovers as voraciously as he enjoyed a good dinner', but despite this, was able to maintain a monumental literary output. Byron's sexual excesses, which included orgies, incest and a steam of prostitutes, lovers, mistresses and young boys, were notorious. Gauguin, who was once kicked unconscious because of the behaviour of his thirteen-year-old mistress, eventually moved to the South Seas, where he reported that his bed was 'invaded every night by young hussies running wild.' Despite this he produced masterpieces that revolutionized modern art.

President Kennedy once admitted that he suffered from severe headaches unless he had a different woman every day, preferably two at a time. Despite this, he managed to be one of the most inspirational statesmen of the twentieth century. Picasso's sexual gluttony was, according to a friend, 'obsessive', but despite a string of mistresses, he was able to complete over fourteen thousand paintings – an amazing output for any artist. And so the list goes on. Stendhal, Toulouse-Lautrec, Van Gogh and Wilde were all attracted to prostitutes and other forms of carnal indulgence, but they were also able to produce great works. Clearly, one way to increase the total sum of happiness is to increase the number of sources from which one derives it.

In addition to carnal and cerebral pursuits, there is also that special kind of physical happiness to be gained from indulging in rhythmic activities such as song, dance, music and the various vertiginous pursuits. Many modern urbanites needlessly give up this type of activity and thereby remove this particular source of happiness from their lives. Few tribal people make this mistake. Any study of tribal societies soon reveals a rich vein of ceremony, celebration and ritual that typically includes rhythmic performances of song, dance, music or movement. In some instances the experiences involved become so intense that the performers seem to enter an almost trancelike state. This is a type of happiness that, in its less extreme versions, is open to anyone as an additional source of physical joy, but because of the insidious spread of screen-watching (cinema, television, computer) is less and less common. In contemporary life, it seems, fantasy-happiness gains are rhythmic-happiness losses.

To some – a suffering minority – there is pleasure to be gained from pain, happiness from denial, and joy from austerity. For others there is a reward to be found in successful risk-taking, where happiness is gained, not from pain, but from pain avoided.

Social life today is increasingly restrictive as regards the number of risks to which people are allowed to expose themselves. Social leaders do their best to instil in their communities the idea that 'safe is best'. Where the risk-taking concerned is unwitting and occurs through ignorance, this is a sound practice, but where it is applied to conscious, delib-erate risk-taking that can harm only the performer, the wisdom of strict social restrictions demands closer scrutiny. If young men, in particular, are biologically programmed to take risks, as they seem to be, then society would do well to provide them with acceptable outlets in order to avoid them taking matters into their own hands and devising unacceptable alternatives. Politically, there is wide scope for increasing the happiness to be gained from the milder forms of risk-taking.

For some citizens, there is an unusually developed ability to ignore the unpleasantness of daily life and to see only the high points. Still others, in complete contrast, become obsessed with the horrors of life and look upon happiness as the rare experience of a cessation of misery.

One solution, in dealing with the trials of life, is to withdraw into an inner state of meditative tranquillity, and to find a form of contemplative happiness there. There has often been the feeling, with this type of happiness, that the meditator must give up his or her active life almost entirely in order to gain the rewards of inner contemplation, but this is not the case. It is possible to obtain tranquil happiness from only occasional bouts of quiet serenity. For those who lead highly stressed lives — overcrowded, over-noisy and over-active — a brief session of contemplation will, from time to time, provide a surprisingly rich source of this unique kind of happiness. If joining a meditation group of some kind is felt to be too 'awkward', there are private ways of obtaining a similar state, even if the process is no more than allowing the brain to go 'off-line' when taking a long, hot bath, or when floating in a swimming pool.

For those who cannot face reality, one popular solution is to escape, either into the chemically induced happiness of drugs, or the fantasy world of fiction. Sadly, almost all known drugs carry a disproportionate cost for the brief spells of happiness they bring, but future research may yet discover a new type of drug that can offer 'highs' without any subsequent 'lows'. Domestic cats, rather surprisingly, have already reached this desirable state. They can gain a condition of ecstasy simply by rolling in a catnip plant, without any unpleasant after-effects. In this respect, rather embarrassingly, they are well in advance of our research chemists.

Finally, there is the unique happiness of the unexpected moment of great good luck. By definition, there is no way we can increase this form of joyful event, except perhaps by buying more lottery tickets.

*

In dealing with each of these types of happiness, I have tried to show that there are not one but many sources that can provide us with this most valuable of mental states. It is not up to me to instruct you as to which type you yourself should attempt to encourage as a way of increasing your total store of happy moments. Some will suit you, some will not. All too often, we set our course in life in a direction that does not suit us, and which brings us only frustration and stress. Seeing all the different ways in which some people have found happiness may, it is hoped, open a new path here and there, and remove, wherever possible, those feelings of guilt that are such enemies of a happy life.

There is one general principle that emerges from an evolutionary study of happiness, and that is that wherever the conditions in which we find ourselves happen to match up with some basic feature of human nature, the chance that moments of happiness will occur is greatly increased. The characteristics I have in mind are such things as curiosity, ambition, competitiveness, helpfulness, sociability, playfulness and imagination — the qualities that, together, make the human species so exciting.

If we live repetitive, dead-end, monotonous lives that deny us our genetic birthright, we may manage to survive and to struggle on from day to day, but we will find ourselves existing in a joyless, miserable state of mind for much of our lifespan. After all, when we put criminals in prison we punish them by giving them precisely this type of existence, removing from them as many sources of happiness as possible.

Sadly, for many law-abiding citizens who have never been in jail, life can be almost as boring. Their daily work-tasks are so repetitive and unimaginative that they simply do not offer any potential for human happiness. Such individuals may not be in prison, but they may nevertheless find themselves confined in the invisible cages of the modern human zoo. If their level of overall happiness is to increase, it can only do so by their taking on a new job or by squeezing all their happy moments into spare-time activities.

Contrary to popular opinion, levels of happiness are not linked to education, age or bank balance. The uneducated are just as able to find happiness as the scholarly. They may find it in different ways, but they will find it. Similarly, the young and the old have their own special ways of being happy – and, for that matter, unhappy. And the rich, it emerges, are only marginally happier than the poor. Even if a rich man has a thousand times more money that a poor one, he will probably only be ten percent happier in his daily life – if that. He may have many more ways of gaining happy moments, but he will be so busy making his money that he will rarely have time to enjoy such moments.

Differences in general levels of happiness seem instead to be much more concerned with differences in individual personalities. In other words, each human being appears to have his or her own 'set-point' level. If the propensity for happiness is registered on a scale of, say, one to ten, then it will be possible to find individuals who register an 'eight' or a 'nine', regardless of what the world throws at them, while others can manage only a 'two' or a 'three', even when everything in life appears to be going well. The first is a cheerful, happy-go-lucky, optimistic extrovert who can find hidden pleasures in almost any situation. The second is a dour, down-in-the-dumps, pessimistic introvert who sees the worst in any situation. If the cheerful type has a bad experience, you know that he will soon bounce back; if the misery has a good experience, you know that he will soon be able to find some fatal flaw in it.

How do these two types arise, and how fixed are they? The answer to the first of these questions can often be found in childhood. The cheerful adult probably had 'Yes' parents and the dour adult probably had 'No' parents. When the child asks the Yes parents 'Can we play a game?' the answer is invariably 'Yes' ('OK. Let's pretend to...'). When the child asks the No parents 'Can we play a game?' the answer is invariably 'No' ('Sorry, I'm too busy to...'). The first child grows up to be positive and to enjoy an active imagination, while the second child comes to accept that life has little joy to offer it.

Such attitudes may appear to be fixed for life, but this is not the case. They may be difficult to shift, but it can be done. If the cheerful person suffers a major trauma, it can cause serious, long-lasting damage. And if the miseries are coached in pleasure-seeking, they can eventually be dragged out of the trough into which they have subsided, thanks to their bad parenting. In other words, parental teachings can leave deep scars (or deep blessings), but they can be modified by later influences in adult life.

For those wishing to increase their score on the happiness scale, the best answer is to refuse to accept that there is only one kind of happiness, and instead to re-examine alternative sources of happiness that are available to them. There may be a rich vein of happiness to be found in some area of life that has never even occurred to them. If this book offers some guidance in directing them to one of those untapped sources, then it will have done its job.

DEFINITIONS OF HAPPINESS

My personal view of happiness, presented in this book, is not the only one. Literally hundreds of definitions of happiness have been recorded over the years, by many original minds. The following is a selection of these, arranged according to the main feature emphasized by each of the authors.

HAPPINESS *is* LIFE'S PURPOSE

A number of authors choose to define the pursuit of happiness as the main obsession of the human race.

Happiness is… the preoccupation of life.
Ruth Benedict

Happiness is the only sanction of life.
George Santayana

Happiness is… all we have time for.
We haven't time to be ourselves.
Albert Camus

Happiness is… the secret motive of all men do.
William James

Happiness is the legal tender of the soul.
R. G. Ingersoll

Happiness is the only good... humanity the only religion.
R. G. Ingersoll

Happiness... of the greatest number is the foundation of morals and legislation.
Jeremy Bentham

Happiness is... the most underrated duty.
Robert Louis Stevenson

Happiness keeps the wheels steadily turning; truth and beauty can't.
Aldous Huxley

Happiness is... the purpose of life.
The Dalai Lama

HAPPINESS *is* AN ATTITUDE

Many authors have made the point that it is the state of mind of the individual that is all-important in obtaining happiness.

Happiness is not the number of blessings, but only our attitude towards them. Alexander Solzhenitsyn

Happiness can be achieved through reshaping our attitudes and outlook. The Dalai Lama

Happiness is not a matter of events; it depends upon the tides of the mind. Alice Meynell

Happiness is in the taste, and not in the things. Duc de la Rochefoucauld

Happiness is... determined more by the state of one's mind than by... events. The Dalai Lama

Happiness depends less on exterior things than most suppose. William Cowper

Happiness can be achieved through the systematic training of our hearts and minds.
The Dalai Lama

Happiness is... knowing that you do not necessarily require happiness. William Saroyan

Happiness is... not the man who seems thus to others, but who seems thus to himself.
Publilius Syrus

Happiness is... the conviction that we are loved for ourselves – loved in spite of ourselves.
Victor Hugo

Happiness will never be any greater than the idea we have of it.
Maurice Maeterlinck

Happiness is itself a kind of gratitude.
Joseph Wood Crutch

Happiness... to some, elation; is to others, mere stagnation. Amy Lowell

Happiness can only be felt if you don't set any condition. Arthur Rubinstein

Happiness is not a reward, it is a consequence.
R. G. Ingersoll

HAPPINESS *is* FLEETING

Several authors have emphasized the brevity of intense happiness.

Happiness is brief. It will not stay.
God batters at its sails. Euripides

Happiness too swiftly flies. Thomas Gray

Happiness makes up in height what it
lacks in length. Robert Frost

Happiness is like a butterfly which appears
and delights us for one brief moment.
Anna Pavlova

Happiness is as smooth as the water on the
verge of the cataract. George Arliss

Happiness is so episodical. Ruth Benedict

Happiness is as beautiful as the rainbow, that
smiling daughter of the storm. George Arliss

Happiness, unbroken, is a bore; it should have
its ups and downs. Molière

HAPPINESS *is* ELUSIVE

A few authors have gone a step further, pointing out that, not only is happiness a fleeting sensation, but that it is also fugitive.

Happiness is like trying to hold water in your hands. Michelangelo Antonioni

Happiness is a goddess in pursuit, but a cloud in possession. George Arliss

Happiness is like a sunbeam, which the least shadow intercepts. Chinese proverb

Happiness is... carried cautiously, like a glass filled to the brim.
Jules Barbey D'Aurevilly

Happiness is... difficult to describe and impossible to dramatize.
Richard Church

Happiness is indeed a Eurydice, vanishing as soon as gazed upon.
Denis de Rougemont

HAPPINESS *is* UNPURSUABLE

Other authors have focused on the fact that happiness cannot be made a goal in itself. It is something that you must find, not seek.

Happiness can be captured only by not pursuing it.
F. L. Lucas

Happiness is not a horse — you cannot harness it.
Russian proverb

Happiness is not best achieved by those who seek it directly. Bertrand Russell

Happiness is... a by-product you get in the process of making something else.
Aldous Huxley

Happiness is... the bird of paradise that alights only on the hand that does not grasp. John Berry

Happiness... comes incidentally. Make it the object of pursuit and it is never attained.
Nathaniel Hawthorne

Happiness, when unsought, is often found.
George Arliss

HAPPINESS *is* IMPOSSIBLE

Other authors go even further, claiming rather pessimistically that, in reality, happiness is an illusion and can never be found under any circumstances — except, possibly, death. One can only wonder at the kind of lives these authors must have led.

Happiness is an imaginary condition,
formerly attributed by the living to the dead.
Thomas Szaz

Happiness can be realized only in heaven.
E. Davies

Happiness is like the statue of Isis, whose veil
no mortal ever raised. W. S. Landor

Happiness is but a dream and sorrow a reality.
Voltaire

Happiness is like the mirage in the desert.
George Arliss

Happiness is a chimaera and suffering a reality.
A. Schopenhauer

Happiness... doesn't exist. Charles de Gaulle

HAPPINESS *is* ACHIEVEMENT

Many authors have selected the human preoccupation with aiming for a long-term goal as a crucial feature of happiness. Several have emphasized that a moderate, achievable goal is better than a lofty, unachievable one. Others dwell on the fact that, with ambitious activities, there is a source of happiness in the anticipation of achievement as well as the final, successful climax.

Happiness is to do a man's true work.
Marcus Aurelius

Happiness is… twelve hours of work on
one occupation. William James

Happiness consists in activity – it is a running
stream, not a stagnant pool. J. M. Good

Happiness is… learning, earning and yearning.
Lillian Gish

Happiness is… knowing that your worst shot
is still going to be pretty good.
American golfer Johnny Miller

Happiness does not lie in happiness, but in the achievement of it. Dostoevsky

Happiness is not a state to arrive at, but a manner of travelling. Margaret Lee Runbeck

Happiness is... to fill the hour, and leave no crevice for a repentance or an approval.
Ralph Waldo Emerson

Happiness is... when a man is willing to be what he is.
Desiderius Erasmus

Happiness is wanting what you get.
Success is getting what you want.
Anonymous

Happiness is a way station between too little and too much. Channing Pollock

Happiness is not having what you want, but wanting what you have. Hyman Schachtel

HAPPINESS *is* VARIED

Among those who do accept that happiness is possible, a few authors have mentioned that it has not one, but a number of different sources.

Happiness… should not be anticipated
from one quarter alone.
Sigmund Freud

Happiness… leads none of us by the
same route.
Charles Caleb Colton

Happiness puts on as many shapes
as discontent.
Phyillis McGinley

Happiness consists in the multiplicity of
agreeable consciousness.
Samuel Johnson

HAPPINESS *is* TO BE FOUND IN TRIVIA

As an extension of the idea that moderate goals are better than unachievable lofty ones, many authors have emphasized the happiness to be found in the trivia of life.

Happiness is to be very busy with the unimportant. Edward Newton

Happiness is… getting immediate and conscious enjoyment from little things. Hugh Walpole

Happiness is in little things. John Ruskin

Happiness springs from temperate habits and simple wishes. James Wood

Happiness is often overlooked because it doesn't cost anything. Anonymous

Happiness is… produced by little advantages that occur every day. Benjamin Franklin

Happiness is… not anticipating too great a happiness. Bernard Le Bovier Fontenelle

HAPPINESS *is*
WINNING

Very few authors mention competitive happiness, and admit that beating rivals can bring feelings of great joy.

Happiness... consists in possessing what others can't get.
H. W. Shaw

Happiness... should not be sought in peace, but in conflict.
Paul Claudel

Happiness is... the feeling that power increases.
Friedrich Nietzsche

Happiness is... not being too concerned with others.
Albert Camus

HAPPINESS *is* SHARED
AND COOPERATIVE

In complete contrast, other authors emphasize a cooperative, caring nature as a source of great happiness.

Happiness that is sought for ourselves
alone can never be found.
Thomas Merton

Happiness is... perceived only when it
is reflected from another.
Samuel Johnson

Happiness is... resigning yourself to seeing
others also happy.
Bertrand Russell

Happiness was born a twin... all who joy would
win, must share it. Lord Byron

Happiness is a great love and much serving.
Olive Schreiner

HAPPINESS *is* SENSUAL

Some authors freely admit to finding happiness, without guilt, in the basic, carnal pleasure of the flesh.

Happiness depends on a leisurely breakfast.
John Gunther

Happiness is fun and food, Kodachromed for later view. Marya Mannes

Happiness is... a good bank account, a good cook, and a good digestion. Jean-Jacques Rousseau

Happiness is... the sublime moment when you get out of your corsets. Joyce Grenfell

Happiness is... driving briskly in a post-chaise with a pretty woman. Samuel Johnson

Happiness is a married woman and a single man.
H. L. Mencken

Happiness is unrepented pleasure. Socrates

Happiness is good health and a bad memory.
Ingrid Bergman

HAPPINESS *is* MATERIALISTIC

Closely related to these hedonistic, carnal statements are the blatant admissions of material things as a main source of happiness.

Happiness is... plenty of property and slaves, with the capacity to get more.
Aristotle

Happiness is... a large income.
Jane Austen

Happiness is... wealth and power.
Gahan Wilson

Happiness, for a man, is... a wife to tell him what to do and a secretary to do it.
Lord Mancroft

HAPPINESS *is* CEREBRAL

Only a very few authors have stressed intellectual activity as a source of happiness, possibly because this source is limited to the intelligent, and to emphasize it makes the authors concerned appear elitist.

Happiness is... to shut yourself up in art, and count everything else as nothing.
Gustave Flaubert

Happiness is a wine of the rarest vintage, and seems insipid to a vulgar taste.
Logan Pearsall Smith

HAPPINESS *is* RATIONALITY

Closely related to the last category is the view that true happiness can be found in the abolition of religion and other superstitious activities, and their replacement with logical, rational thought.

Happiness (of the people) is the abolition of religion.
Karl Marx

Happiness is... not believing in miracles.
Johann Wolfgang von Goethe

HAPPINESS *is* NEGATIVE

Some authors, viewing the world bleakly, have emphasized the negative view that happiness is to be found merely in the cessation of one's own unhappiness, or in the contemplation of the unhappiness of others.

Happiness is the interval between
periods of unhappiness.
Don Marquis

Happiness is... the occasional episode
in the general drama of pain.
Thomas Hardy

Happiness is composed of misfortunes avoided.
Alphonse Karr

Happiness is not being pained in body or
troubled in mind.
Thomas Jefferson

HAPPINESS *is* TRANQUILLITY

For the over-stressed, or those devoted to a meditational form of lifestyle, the key to happiness is to be found in peace and quiet.

Happiness is... an enemy to pomp and noise.
Joseph Addison

Happiness would be to be alone at the seaside
and then be left in peace.
Louis-Ferdinand Céline

Happiness is a tranquil acquiescence under
an agreeable delusion.
Laurence Sterne

Happiness... consists in tranquillity of mind.
Cicero

Happiness is... neither wealth nor splendour,
but tranquillity and occupation.
Thomas Jefferson

HAPPINESS *is* INNOCENCE

*Certain authors have concluded that a sophisticated, complex
lifestyle makes it difficult to find happiness. For them, the only
answer is the simplicity of an innocent.*

Happiness is above all things the calm,
glad certainty of innocence.
Henrik Ibsen

Happiness is innocence.
Marguerite Yourcenar

Happiness is… a clear conscience.
Edward Gibbon

HAPPINESS *is* STUPIDITY

To some authors, however, innocence is the equivalent of ignorance and therefore stupidity, and they see the 'innocence of happiness' in a more critical light.

Happiness and intelligence are so seldom found in the same person.
William Feather

Happiness is... the serene and peaceful state of being a fool among knaves.
Jonathan Swift

Happiness is the exploration and enjoyment of genius untainted by one's own lack of it.
Benedict Spinoza

Happiness is... a combination of heredity, health, good fortune and shallow intellect.
Arthur Marshall

Happiness makes us base.
John Marston

HAPPINESS is
FANTASY

A few authors have mentioned escape from reality as a main source of happiness.

Happiness is... getting out of oneself,
and staying out.
Henry James

Happiness depends on the energy to assume
the mask of some other self.
W. B. Yeats

Happiness... resides in things unseen.
Edward Young

HAPPINESS *is* IRRATIONAL
AND IMAGINATIVE

Related to the idea of happiness-through-fantasy is the concept of happiness obtained by exercising the imagination.

Happiness is not an ideal of reason but of imagination. Immanuel Kant

Happiness is a mystery like religion and should never be rationalized.
G. K. Chesterton

Happiness resides in imaginative reflection and judgement.
George Santayana

HAPPINESS *is* A MATTER OF LUCK

Surprisingly, hardly anyone has picked on the element of chance in bringing moments of happiness. There appears to be only one single quotation with this in mind:

Happiness is probably only a passing accident.
Anonymous

HAPPINESS – UNCLASSIFIED

Finally, there are also a number of definitions of happiness that are unclassifiable. A few of the best of these are as follows:

Happiness is no laughing matter.
Richard Whately

Happiness is… is not hearing the clock strike.
German proverb

Happiness is… accepting change gracefully.
James Stewart

Happiness is a ball after which we run wherever it rolls. Johann Wolfgang von Goethe

Happiness is white and pink. Théophile Gautier

Happiness is… an uninhibited hypothalamus.
P. T. Young

Happiness is… a kind of daylight in the mind.
Joseph Addison

Happiness never lays its finger on its pulse.
Alexander Smith

And, as a tailpiece...

> In Hollywood, if you don't have
> happiness, you send out for it.
> Rex Reed